OVERTO
UNDERCURRENTS

"Warning: Do not read this book if you are committed to limiting your reality to the Western scientific bias. However, do read this book if you are open to realizing that certain aspects of consciousness found in almost every society throughout history truly do exist. The moving and well-told case histories and short flashes of therapeutic breakthrough illustrate clear benefits of going beyond the Western paradigm. Without preaching or scolding, Metzner gives example after example of how much more a therapist can accomplish using tools developed and refined by other cultures. Better yet, Metzner describes the tools in full detail and how he uses them so that we are not only enlightened but empowered. Reading this book will loosen your own boundaries, let you reflect on the practical value of opening up to other realities, and surprise you with how easily and how quickly people can dissolve previously intractable pathology when guided to accessing and using altered states."

JAMES FADIMAN, PH.D., MICRODOSE RESEARCHER AND
AUTHOR OF *THE PSYCHEDELIC EXPLORER'S GUIDE:
SAFE, THERAPEUTIC, AND SACRED JOURNEYS*

"A most welcome addition to the highly influential and gifted scholarship of Ralph Metzner's vibrant life work. This erudite set of well-documented case studies profoundly illuminates the empowerment and healing to be evoked through a masterful weaving of psychedelic medicines, invocations, and divinations. As a genius alchemist of consciousness, Metzner successfully challenges erroneous accepted worldviews with insights into both how karmic undercurrents of suffering persist across generations and how close we are to healing through the powerful practices he has developed and deftly illustrated here. So potent are these insights, the reading of this visionary book is an act of receiving the vital medicine it describes."

JANIS PHELPS, PH.D., CLINICAL PSYCHOLOGIST, PROFESSOR, AND
DIRECTOR OF THE CENTER FOR PSYCHEDELIC THERAPIES AND RESEARCH
AT THE CALIFORNIA INSTITUTE OF INTEGRAL STUDIES

"Legendary transpersonal psychologist Ralph Metzner's deeply compelling, page-turning stories will keep your eyes glued to this one-of-a-kind book. Metzner writes with great clarity, insight, and profound knowledge. This book provides the instructions for re-creating the alchemically transformative, conscious-altering explorations that reveal possible influences from past incarnations and ancestral spirits. Metzner recounts 15 thought-provoking case histories that will surprise and instruct the curious mind as well as help those in need of psychotherapeutic assistance. With its abundance of rare knowledge, this extraordinary book can help to put much unexplained phenomena into perspective, so as to become more comprehensible, more manageable, and to help facilitate a deep healing process."

DAVID JAY BROWN, AUTHOR OF *DREAMING WIDE AWAKE* AND *THE NEW SCIENCE OF PSYCHEDELICS*

"Ralph Metzner draws on his intuitive understanding of the subtleties and varieties of psychedelic experience as he recounts these very human stories of spiritual healing and family reconciliation across time and space."

DON LATTIN, AUTHOR OF *THE HARVARD PSYCHEDELIC CLUB* AND *CHANGING OUR MINDS*

"Ralph Metzner is a modern Western medicine man. His knowledge in his extraordinary stories is to be savored again and again, encouraging us to become spiritually aroused. In a larger sense, Metzner is a spiritual statesman. . . . You will enjoy this wonderful book, and your soul will be immeasurably enhanced in response."

HANK WESSELMAN PH.D., ANTHROPOLOGIST AND AUTHOR OF *THE RE-ENCHANTMENT* AND THE *SPIRITWALKER* TRILOGY

"Ralph Metzner has done it again! Each of his books expands the domain of human knowledge and explores neglected aspects of human potential. In *Overtones and Undercurrents,* he tells his readers what he has discovered as a psychotherapist who incorporates psychedelics, reincarnation, and spirituality into his work with clients. Each case history reads like a novella; in addition to his skill as a therapist, Metzner is a superb storyteller."

STANLEY KRIPPNER, PH.D., COAUTHOR OF *PERSONAL MYTHOLOGY*

OVERTONES *AND* UNDERCURRENTS

Spirituality, Reincarnation, *and* Ancestor Influence *in* Entheogenic Psychotherapy

RALPH METZNER, Ph.D.

Park Street Press
Rochester, Vermont • Toronto, Canada

Park Street Press
One Park Street
Rochester, Vermont 05767
www.ParkStPress.com

Text stock is SFI certified

Park Street Press is a division of Inner Traditions International

Library of Congress Cataloging-in-Publication Data

Names: Metzner, Ralph, author.
Title: Overtones and undercurrents : spirituality, reincarnation, and ancestor influence in entheogenic psychotherapy / Ralph Metzner, Ph.D.
Description: Rochester, Vermont : Park Street Press, [2017] | Includes bibliographical references and index.
Identifiers: LCCN 2017003355 (print) | LCCN 2017018838 (e-book) | ISBN 9781620556894 (paperback) | ISBN 9781620556900 (e-book)
Subjects: LCSH: Psychotherapy—Religious aspects. | Spiritual healing. | Spirituality. | Mind and body. | BISAC: PSYCHOLOGY / Movements / Transpersonal. | BODY, MIND & SPIRIT / Spirituality / Shamanism.
Classification: LCC RC489.S676 (e-book) | LCC RC489.S676 M48 2017 (print) | DDC 616.89/14—dc23
LC record available at https://lccn.loc.gov/2017003355

Printed and bound in the United States by Lake Book Manufacturing, Inc. The text stock is SFI certified. The Sustainable Forestry Initiative® program promotes sustainable forest management.

10 9 8 7 6 5 4 3 2 1

Text design and layout by Priscilla Baker
This book was typeset in Garamond Premier Pro with Helvetica Neue and Grota Sans used as display typefaces

To send correspondence to the author of this book, mail a first-class letter to the author c/o Inner Traditions • Bear & Company, One Park Street, Rochester, VT 05767, and we will forward the communication, or contact the author directly at **www.greenearthfound.org**.

Contents

◆ ◆ ◆

Introduction

*O*vertones are the subtle sounds created in stringed instruments by the sympathetic vibrations of the struck or plucked fundamental strings. To the listener the sounds are ethereal, as if floating above the sound of the fundamental note. Overtones are also heard in the vocal chanting of Tibetan and Mongolian overtone singers, who are able to lower their natural bass tone to produce these ethereal sounds. We can think of the spiritual dimensions of our experience, which we refer to as "spirit" or "soul," as analogous to these subtle floating sounds. They are the inner tones and subtle harmonics of spirit and soul that can accompany our experience in certain mystical and spiritual states when we become sensitized to them.

Undercurrents are the invisible flows of water below the surface that can induce powerful movements of objects on the surface in unexpected and even dangerous directions—toward damaging rocks or abysmal depths. Analogously, the karmic entanglements of past incarnations can affect our present experience with seemingly unfounded feelings of guilt, indebtedness, resentment, or shame. To resolve them safely requires attending to the subsurface psychic currents in our life until we can recognize these residual patterns and take the appropriate steps to heal them.

The recognition of higher spiritual dimensions and the acknowledgment of karmic residuals are occult and taboo subjects for Westerners raised within the dominant materialist worldview. However, the basic concepts, with natural cultural variations, are accepted as a matter of course in Eastern and indigenous societies. It was only with the rise of the transpersonal psychology and psychotherapy movement during the 1970s that we had the beginnings of an ongoing revision of the materialist paradigm and the development of psychotherapeutic practices that recognize the reality of the spiritual dimensions and their connection to our quest for healing and sanity.

A broader new worldview emerged—and is still emerging—that could accommodate experiences and practices involving psychedelics but also nondrug approaches to consciousness expansion incorporating mindfulness meditation, holotropic breathwork, shamanic journeying methods, intentional conscious dreaming, and a variety of expressive art forms involving music, movement, mandala drawing, and others. The new paradigm formulations using "transpersonal" concepts have the advantage of being applicable across different religious traditions, both Eastern and Western. They allow practitioners of the new therapies to communicate with one another while avoiding entanglement in theological or doctrinal specifics of different religions.

I first became acquainted with the use of psychedelics to explore nonordinary realms of consciousness through my participation in the psychedelic drug studies at Harvard University in the early 1960s, with Tim Leary and Richard Alpert, who later became known as Ram Dass. We had followed a suggestion of Aldous

Huxley and adapted the teachings of the Tibetan Book of the Dead as the basis for our guidebook on psychedelic states, *The Psychedelic Experience,* first published in 1964. The continuing popularity of our adaptation of this core Buddhist text attests to the value and relevance of the principles of karma and reincarnation, as well as teachings concerning higher dimensions, to the mind-expanding experiences people were having with psychedelics.

The research into psychedelic substances and their possible uses in psychotherapy made it abundantly clear that the drugs, per se, do not produce or cause experiences of insight and healing. Rather, they function as amplifiers and intensifiers of perceptual awareness, which can be profoundly healing when taken in a supportive setting but can also be disorienting and confusing in unprepared situations. Psychedelic experiences are always a function of the intention, or "set," of the individual, and the "setting," or context, as well as the preparation done beforehand. Because such drugs and related plants and fungi amplify and vivify perception, they have functioned for many people, including myself, as a first mind-opening foray into the realms of prebirth, after-death, other-world, and past-life experience.

Recognizing the importance of a meditative approach to drug-induced altered states had obvious implications for arranging the set and setting for individuals who had confusing experiences as a result of the disorganized and careless use of mind-altering drugs. In the late 1960s, I was working as a psychologist at what was then Mendocino State Hospital in Talmage, Northern California. While working at the state hospital I had the opportunity to apply some of the lessons my colleagues and I had learned about the importance of a peaceful environment to help someone lost in drug-induced inner space explorations. In chapter 1, "Finding Inner Stillness in a Place of Madness," I relate the story of how I set up a quiet, darkened meditation chamber in the mental hospital that helped a young man sort out the inner chaos into which he had fallen through naively careless ingestion of street drugs.

During the past forty years, as I developed my practice of individual and group psychotherapy, using entheogenic amplification when possible and refraining from the use of such substances when circumstances did not permit it, I was continuously integrating yogic meditative practices and perspectives into my work. I spent most of the 1970s immersed in the intensive study of the *agni yoga* light-fire energy practices, taught in the School of Actualism. Inheriting and reactivating the traditions of Eastern and Western alchemy, these methods use concentration to tap into inner sources of healing, expanding awareness of the subtle energy fields at different levels of mind, feeling, and body and dissolving blockages by using the purifying action of inner fire.

In my work with individuals, as related in the stories in this book, I practiced and taught the light-fire meditation practices for attunement to the spiritual realms, using language that was neutral with regard to specific religious systems. I would verbalize prayer-like invocations of healing and helping spirits, especially those with whom the client already had a connection through previous practice. Sometimes, when circumstances permitted, small amounts of an entheogenic substance could be used to amplify the client's perception during the guided divinations. Rhythmic rattling would also be used at times to initiate and support the therapeutic dialogues with the client's higher, guiding self.

In such a mindfully prepared and protected state, connections and communications with deceased ancestors and healing deity spirits can take place that go far beyond what is normally possible.

The client and I remain in constant contact through a question-and-answer divination process in which questions are posed and the answers received from the spirits are verbalized.

Among the most useful integrative practices is the construction and use of a circular diagram with a fourfold cross known as a "medicine wheel" among North American indigenous people and as a "mandala" in the Asian Hindu and Buddhist traditions. Such diagrams, which exist in countless variations, are considered symbols of four main dimensions of one's life, such as the four directions in our environment, the four elements, the four parts of the psyche, the four main roles in a family, and many others. C. G. Jung and psychotherapists working in his lineage have used mandala drawings as expressions of a fourfold map of the psyche, which can provide profound healing insights into the transformative process.

From my own studies of Jung and his mapping of the psyche, as well as my studies of the indigenous medicine wheel principles, I developed a process of inner attunement and integration I call the Medicine Wheel of Spirit Guides, or Four Gateways of Being. I have used this quaternity in my work with individuals, as well as in groups. From the two polarities of male and female and youth and old age we generate a fourfold process of attunement to these four great archetypes that exist within each of us. I describe this process and how it led to a surprising teaching about intimacy and relationships in chapter 2, "Guidance on Intimacy Received from the Goddess Artemis."

◆ ◆ ◆

The next two chapters deal with the topic of healing the residual after-effects of difficult circumstances in the prenatal period. Mainstream psychology and psychiatry, locked into a materialist worldview, do not give any credence to prenatal memories, much less memories of the soul's choice before and around conception. Nevertheless, once we allow our conceptual prejudices to be suspended with an attitude of radical empiricism, we find that vivid memories from before birth, from the circumstances around conception, and from the soul's choice of incarnation can have profound effects on the individual. In my practice I have often found myself working with memory imprints from birth or from prenatal existence, which can be intentionally accessed by guided attunement, with or without psychedelic amplification.

The two stories presented here deal with the sensitive issue of abortion and its consequences. Even those who, like myself, respect absolutely the moral right of a woman to choose whether or not to carry a fetus to term cannot ignore the serious psychological difficulties that can sometimes occur with pregnancies not carried to term. I have had several occasions in my practice to facilitate a soul communication between a mother or father and their aborted child, analogous to that which can occur between any living soul and their deceased relative. The basic fact is that although the body, the soul's vehicle, may die—before, during, or long after birth—the soul cannot be aborted; it is immortal. When the death of a fetus is intentionally brought about before birth, for whatever reason, there may be unexpected consequences—which can, however, also be healed and resolved.

Chapter 3, "Vicissitudes of the Soul on the Journey to a Human Birth," concerns a therapeutic divination I conducted with a woman in her forties who had had an abortion more than twenty years before. When we were going through a forgiveness and healing process with the unborn soul of her aborted child, we were interrupted by a clear telepathic communication from a young man who identified himself as the contentedly reincarnated soul of the child the woman had aborted many years before.

In chapter 4, "Longing for the Twin Soul Left Behind in Heaven," I relate the story of a young man who was conceived and born to a mother who had recently aborted a set of twins. Filled with remorse, the mother had then given birth to a son who was haunted all his life by the sense that he was the reincarnation of one of the aborted twins and that he had a "twin sister left behind in heaven." Recognizing this connection enabled the young man to stop searching for the embodiment of his idealized twin sister and instead develop a realistic relationship with a potential partner.

Chapter 5, "Spider Grandmother Heals the Effects of Childhood Sexual Abuse," recounts the dramatic story of a woman physician, with a personal history of childhood sexual abuse, who unexpectedly found herself in an intimate healing relationship with Grandmother Spider, the Creator and healing spirit for many of the Pueblo Indians of the American Southwest, with whom she was previously totally unfamiliar. The profound visionary experience and connection to a personal totemic spirit guide took place in the context of a group ceremony with entheogenic amplification.

◆ ◆ ◆

The next three stories illustrate the value and importance of recognizing and acknowledging ancestral soul connections. When working with issues around familial, parental, and ancestral relations, the client and I together co-create a kind of family soul council. We respectfully invite all members of the family to a gathering in inner space to confer on a matter of interest and concern to all. The family council of souls includes all those related by birth and genetic ancestry and those related by marriage and the coparenting of children. And since souls are immortal, a meeting of the soul council includes all those who are already "on the other side." People are often astounded to discover that they can have profound and meaningful meetings and conversations on a soul level with family members and ancestors they never knew personally, or that have been dead for a long time. What develops then is a kind of multigenerational conversation in the context of a family council, in which hidden aspects of the family matrix, both positive and negative, can be revealed and conflicts healed.

Chapter 6, "Family Reconciliation through an Indigenous Ancestor," relates the story of a man who discovered that he had a deep spiritual bond with an indigenous ancestor, his mother's father, previously unsuspected. As he remembered and acknowledged this ancestral connection he was able to resolve long-persisting tensions with his parents.

In chapter 7, "Releasing the Daughter from Her Father's Youthful Tragic Obsession," I relate the story of a woman who found that her long-deceased father's secret unrequited love (which occurred before her birth) had blocked her from developing her own love life. This was an example of how the recognition and acknowledgment of parental and ancestral entanglements can enable the resolution of long-held blockages.

Chapter 8, "A Message of Peace Sent by a Dying Man to His Daughter," recounts the story of a woman whose father died in a plane crash when she was in her mother's womb. The mother never recovered from the shock of seeming abandonment and never acknowledged to her daughter the relationship with the father. In the course of healing divinations the woman was able to connect with the soul of her long-deceased father, who had reached out to her child-self in her dreams.

◆ ◆ ◆

To consider reports from prenatal or preconception parental experiences as possible sources of personal difficulties and hence potential new avenues of knowledge and understanding requires us to suspend the prejudices of the generally accepted worldview of our culture and community. Even more remote from the accepted paradigms, at least in Western culture, are experiences of remembering and tracking past incarnations, with potential insights into the karmic projects and entanglements of the soul. In most Asian societies, a much deeper acceptance and understanding of the soul and of reincarnation are reflected in numerous myths and spiritual writings.

My own experience has confirmed what the literature on past-lives psychotherapy suggests: karmic fixations on unresolved difficulties occur most often when the death in the past life was unexpected, unprepared for, or attended with violent emotions. This is consistent with the teachings of Books of the Dead in various cultures that emphasize mindfulness and meditative preparation for the final passage.

It is impossible to exaggerate the profoundly healing significance of experiencing conscious communication with a deceased beloved relative—something the mainstream Western worldview regards as impossible or occult speculation. Because of my own experience of learning to communicate meaningfully and repeatedly with my son who died in an accident as a child, I am able to convey my experience-based conviction, rather than mere belief, that such communication is indeed possible. This is not to say that communication with a deceased loved one always or automatically happens for survivors, but openness to the possibility increases the survivors' receptivity to such communication.

I have been repeatedly impressed, in doing this work on the vicissitudes of the soul around matters of life and death, by the flexibility and creativity of the choices that souls seem able to make in relation to incarnation in a human family. I have observed, although I do not know if it is always true, that when a child or young person dies, which is contrary to the natural cycle of family life, the departed soul may be moved to incarnate again into the same family, as if wanting to complete an agreement among several souls to make a family together. In the normal course of events, it appears that souls discarnate when the person has completed their natural life cycle. They may then go on to incarnate again, after a time, into another society and a different family with different conditions, perhaps even as the opposite gender, always seeking to maximize learning and growth with the healing power of unconditional love.

The following four stories illustrate how the recognition and tracking of the soul's past lives can help resolve underlying difficulties in the present.

In chapter 9, "The Lost Beloved Brother Returned as the Son," I relate the story of a man who, through the divination process we were doing to connect with the council of ancestral souls, discovered that he was the reincarnation of his father's beloved older brother, who had died when the father was a young boy. This story illustrates the perhaps rare occurrence of reincarnation into the same family. This man's past-life regression to a warrior's life of battle and tragic loss provided a deeper spiritual perspective to the difficulties in his present life.

Chapter 10, "Releasing Guilt in the Healing Temple of Justice," tells the story of a man who was plagued by flashbacks to a past life in which he was the mayor of a small town in Czechoslovakia that was invaded by the German army in 1939. In that life he was induced to reveal to the Germans the names of resistance fighters, including his own sons, on the promise that their lives would be spared. The promise was broken and everyone, including the mayor, was massacred. He died consumed by guilt and rage at the betrayal. In the healing divination we went to the ancestral council of immortal souls, where the inner karmic significance of each life and the choices made could be recognized, accepted, and healed.

In chapter 11, "A Mother's Past-Life Deathbed Vow Carried Over," I relate the story of a woman who had a strange compulsion, even as a child, to take care of her father's material needs. She traced this to a past life in which she was the impoverished unmarried mother of a disabled son (her present-life father) and had made a deathbed vow that she would always take care of him. Many mythic stories confirm the karmic holding power of vows, whether of love or revenge, that are made at the moment of death.

In chapter 12, "The Liberating Death of a Persecuted Witch Healer," a woman who was plagued by a repetitive past-life nightmare of persecution by a murderous mob was freed when she recognized and accepted that the terrifying death had actually occurred—and she saw that she was immediately afterward reunited with her beloved family of souls.

◆ ◆ ◆

Of all the experiences reported by participants in my alchemical divination ceremonial groups, possession states provide the most radical challenges to the generally accepted worldview of the modern Western world. This modern worldview does not accept "possession" as a real phenomenon, although serious clinical research and writing have been done on the topic in other countries, especially Brazil.

In chapter 13, "A Ceremony of Depossession from a Malignant Intrusion," I describe a therapeutic group ceremony with a short-acting psychoactive medicine during which a strange state of possession occurred in one of the participants. Although she was in a state of distress that was obvious to all, the woman was able to describe what was happening to her as the possession took hold. The possession state was neutralized with the conscious intervention of and support by myself and the rest of the group.

In chapter 14, "Converting a Possessing Entity into a Protective Ally," I relate the experience of a psychiatrist who had been treating a patient with an apparent case of demonic possession. In the course of some group sessions with psychedelics he found himself possessed by the same entity that was afflicting his patient. Working collaboratively he and I improvised an exorcism using alchemical, shamanic, and spiritual self-defense techniques and were successful in permanently disconnecting the possessing entity from the psychiatrist, as well as from his unfortunate patient in absentia.

In relating these experiences from the paradigm borderlands of current psychological and psychiatric practice, my aim is to demonstrate that an expanded understanding and recognition of prenatal and karmic factors, as well as reincarnational and possession influences, will contribute to deeper and more complete healing processes. In our time of worldwide social and environmental catastrophes, we can ill afford to ignore the wisdom and healing knowledge from other times and other cultures that can help us alleviate both physical and psychological suffering.

In chapter 15, "The Healing Wisdom of the Serpent," I describe healing ceremonies that involved the use of serpentine imagery to guide the psycho-spiritual-somatic process. Experiences with three different serpentine imagery processes are described: the *ouroboros* serpent used in Chinese Taoist practices; the single-serpent staff associated with *Asclepius,* the Greek god of healing; and the double-serpent staff associated with *Hermes,* the deity of wisdom and communication. The results obtained with these methods demonstrate that the symbolic images of the healer's art, at a deeper, esoteric level, depict experiential healing techniques. Practicing them in that way, with mild entheogenic amplification, can bring about new insights and understandings, thereby reconnecting us with these millennia-old traditions of healing and wisdom.

1

Finding Inner Stillness in a Place of Madness

In the mid-1960s, I moved to San Francisco from the East Coast where I was living in an intentional community in Millbrook, New York. I was part of a vast movement of psychedelic pioneers and hippie pilgrims seeking a new paradise in the West. "California Dreaming" and "All You Need Is Love" were among the anthems of this movement, playing constantly on the radio. Tens of thousands of young people and some older ones as well moved westward with blithe assurance and yet incredulity that a new age of peace and love was at hand. "California is love," said one seventeen-year-old hitch-hiking girl with ecstatic confidence.

The Millbrook community, formally known as the Castalia Foundation, consisted of Timothy Leary and his two children, Richard Alpert, my wife Susan and me, among a dozen or so others in a constantly changing cast of characters. Ram Dass and I, along with coauthor Gary Bravo, have recently written about our life in this community in *Birth of a Psychedelic Culture* (2010). Those of us living there, along with the numerous other weekend visitors, were constantly meeting and talking and doing sessions with not-yet-illegal psychedelic substances, trying to figure out where this "movement" was taking us. The weekend public seminars we conducted (without drugs) and the occasional donations we received were ridiculously insufficient to pay the escalating expenses of the community, and the credit card debts mounted relentlessly. Nobody in the community had a paying "job."

Eventually I obtained a publisher's advance of $2,000, a considerable sum in those days, to write and edit *The Ecstatic Adventure* (1968), my first collection of psychedelic experience reports. The money enabled me and three other friends to drive a Volkswagen van from New York to San Francisco. We had several cardboard boxes filled with copies of the first two issues of our quarterly journal, *The Psychedelic Review,* which we dropped off at various New Age bookstores along the way, hoping they would sell.

Generous friends and supporters on the way offered us beds to sleep in, food to eat, and enthusiastic confidence that a new age was indeed at hand. When we arrived in San Francisco, I was able to stay in Berkeley at Timothy Leary's old house, where he had lived during the 1950s. Our little community, like so many others at that time, was consciously sharing income and expenses, so I didn't pay Tim any rent—but I still needed income for all other expenses.

Through my friendship and connection with Robert Mogar, a psychology professor at San Francisco State University and a supporter of our Millbrook-based writing and publishing projects, I obtained a contract to give a series of lectures on the psychopharmacology of psychedelic drugs to the staff at Mendocino State Hospital. The popular casual-tripping use of these drugs was on the rise, and psychiatric clinics and hospitals were beginning to see "bad trip" casualties requiring pharmacological intervention and at times temporary hospitalization.

Mendocino State Hospital was a sprawling campus built in 1889 as a hospital for the "criminally insane." By the late 1950s it had a resident patient population of three thousand chronic psychotics and alcoholics and several progressive treatment programs and innovative staff-training programs. This was in the era before the newer medications, and the treatment drug of choice for psychosis was Thorazine, which had the disconcerting side effect of turning patients' skin a blotchy purple color. A couple of days a week, I conducted training programs for the staff in meditation techniques as well as psychopharmacology courses. I would stay in one of the guest cottages on the hospital grounds and I remember sometimes being woken at night by the bloodcurdling screams of poor souls tormented by their inner dream demons. When I was offered a full-time position as a clinical psychologist at the hospital, I was glad to be able to move off campus to a more tranquil location.

My position at the state hospital lasted only about two years, and the hospital itself was closed in 1972. Five years later the facilities were purchased by a Chinese/Vietnamese Buddhist community and reopened as the City of Ten Thousand Buddhas, one of the largest Buddhist monastic communities in the West. It includes a main temple hall with ten thousand gold-painted Buddha statues, strict Vinaya monasteries for men and separate ones for women, as well as extensive educational programs for children, teens, and adults. It somehow seems to me to be a karmic turn of good fortune that Buddhist monks and nuns have come into this environment to cleanse and purify it of the negative vibrations left by the unfortunate insane from previous generations.

◆ ◆ ◆

In my research and reading on the psychological effects of psyche-delics, I had become impressed by the observations and theorizing of people like the English psychiatrist Humphrey Osmond, the man who first gave mescaline to Aldous Huxley in the mid-1950s. Huxley had formulated the metaphor of the human mind functioning nor-mally as a kind of "reducing valve" that constrained the inherent pro-fusion of sensory influx to a manageable size for daily functioning. In psychotic states such as schizophrenia, this reducing filter was turned off, as was the ability to distinguish inner images from outer percep-tions. The individual was therefore overwhelmed by a profusion of thoughts and images and unable to test the reality of the perceptions and conceptions streaming through his mind—especially in the ini-tial or "psychotic break" phase, before the strange new perceptions congealed into a more fixed delusional system.

According to this line of thought, LSD and other psychedelics also suspended the action of this inhibitory mechanism temporarily, resulting in an enormous influx of amplified sense impressions in all modalities and intensified perception of interior images and thought forms. My experience with psychedelic hallucinations helped me to understand the psychotic dilemma. On a trip with a psychedelic drug you could hear voices or see strange visual distortions, but they were fleeting and you could usually move your attention beyond them to other aspects of your experience, provided you were in a calm, pro-tected setting. You always had the memory of having taken a drug that started this unusual state. The unfortunate madman had no such memory or knowledge and was left to speculate on how these strange perceptions had come about.

The individual on a psychotic "trip" might be tuned in to a voice he could not turn off or see visual distortions he could not control. It was like having a radio receiver stuck on a certain channel that one could not change. Furthermore, most of the voices were repeating messages of a derisive and degrading character—e.g., "you stupid idiot . . . it's all your fault . . . she hates you . . . you're crazy," and so on. Most significantly, the individual did not have the reassuring knowledge that this was a drug-induced trip that would, probably and hopefully, end.

Humphrey Osmond theorized that in naturally occurring psychotic states, the normal perceptual inhibitors had also been suspended, due to some biochemical quirk in the brain. Experimental measurement had confirmed a lowering of perceptual thresholds in psychotic states, similar to that in psychedelic states. If a person suddenly found themselves tasting all the subtle flavors in their food because of this unrecognized heightened sensitivity, they might attribute it to something unusual having been added. From there it would not be a big step, for those with a suspicious predisposition, to think that the food had been poisoned. Others, perceiving unusual sensations in their heads, might understandably be led to speculate that they had somehow been "wired" by something or someone in their environment. It had been observed that schizophrenics often seemed to incorporate the latest technology in their delusions—they had X-ray hallucinations, nuclear radiation fantasies, laser beam paranoias, computer "bugs," and so forth.

One corollary to the lowering of sensitivity thresholds in psychotic, as in psychedelic, states is that the individual could become telepathic to the thoughts of others without recognizing it. This was demonstrated to me one time at the Mendocino State Hospital when I was sitting in the admissions center next to a schizophrenic girl who babbled a constant, incoherent stream of verbiage—what psychiatry technically refers to as "word salad." As I was listening to this outpouring of seemingly nonsensical verbiage, I began to notice that my own unexpressed associations to what she was saying were also appearing, with a slight delay, in her verbal mix. I realized that, unbeknownst to her, her brain had turned into an intermittent telepathic receiver and was picking up the thoughts of others in her environment and mixing them with her own thoughts. This was terrifying to her because of her inability to control or stop it or to distinguish her own thoughts from those of others. She was reacting with rage and confusion to the negative, insane, and random ideas flying through her head from those around her. No wonder that schizophrenic patients often complain that "the people here are driving me crazy."

A practical consequence of these notions for both psychedelic and schizophrenic expansions of consciousness was that such experiences should ideally occur in a calm, peaceful setting, akin to a monastery or rural retreat center, so that the amplified multiplicity of sense perceptions and unrecognized telepathic thought transfer would be less likely to overwhelm the individual. This line of thought also correlated with the research that was beginning to show that reducing the intensity and variety of external sense stimulation led to an expanded and deepened state of consciousness by itself, without any drugs or other input.

During this period in the early 1960s, the *sensory deprivation* or *sensory isolation* chamber research of John Lilly and others was attracting attention. Simple quiet environments, low in noise and visual variety, appeared to naturally produce or support a peaceful, calm state in ordinary individuals. The extreme end of such installations is the *samadhi* tank, in which one floats in a warm salt water solution, dissolving the difference between inner and outer sensations. Conversely, some people had suggested that being in that kind of sensory isolation environment, similar to a monastic meditation chamber, could possibly help someone in the throes of a psychotic experience, allowing them to gradually accommodate and process the greater input from internal sources.

With these observations and speculations in mind, I requested and received permission from the hospital administration to construct a simplified sensory deprivation or meditation chamber. The room held only a mattress on a cot, was totally dark, and, though it was impossible to create complete silence in the large hospital building, was relatively quiet. I offered a stay in the chamber to patients going through any kind of psychotic or just confusing episode, as a totally optional, freely chosen experience. No one was ever put in the chamber against their wishes or as a kind of punishment, nor was the room ever locked—people could freely come and go. Ahead of time, I fully explained that the intent and purpose behind the experience was to allow the person in the chamber a period of respite from the flood of external visual and auditory input. The technical staff, at my request, had set up an intercom system, so that the person in the room could speak, and their verbalizations could be listened to and recorded. I was sitting outside the room and could respond to any questions that were asked, but otherwise stayed quiet. The following story occurred in this setting.

The Story of Tom: An Outcast Seeking Refuge

After I had started to work as a full-time psychologist at the Mendocino State Hospital, I was sometimes asked to consult on cases of "bad trip" reactions to psychedelics that were brought up from the Haight-Ashbury district in San Francisco when hospitalization was deemed necessary. Sometime in 1968 a young man (whom I shall call "Tom") was admitted to the emergency room in a psychotic-like state, apparently triggered by his LSD experiences. He had been living in the Haight-Ashbury district of San Francisco in a commune with a fluctuating number of residents for about a year and had ingested an unknown amount of LSD. His behavior over a period of two months had become progressively more disturbing to his friends. Although he was never violent and ate and slept regularly, his communication and contact with others had increasingly deteriorated. He seemed to be in a state of worsening anxiety and confusion and did not participate in activities with others, increasingly becoming a concern for his friends. One of these friends knew of my work with LSD and persuaded him to come up to the emergency clinic at the hospital to seek help. I was told he had agreed to come since he knew my name, but it was not clear whether he anticipated "treatment."

In 1969 I wrote a paper titled "A Note on the Treatment of LSD Psychosis: A Case Report," which was subsequently published in *Psychotherapy: Theory, Research and Therapy.* In this paper I introduced the notion that the so-called bad trip phenomena that could occur with psychedelics when they were ingested in a careless manner, with minimal attention to a positive set and setting, needed to be addressed in a way that could retrieve and retain the positive possibilities of the experience. The following passages are from that paper.

> His physical appearance on arrival was somewhat uncared for—
> "hippie" shirt and beads, hair almost touching his shoulders. He
> held his hands in front of him clasped in such a way that the
> fingers were pulling against each other sideways. His eyes were
> darting around anxiously, his mouth smiling or laughing rather
> frequently in a fearful, excited manner. He would talk in a low
> voice, much of which was inaudible. His whole face twitched and

jerked so that his glasses moved up and down on his nose, and from time to time his eyes would roll inward, to the nose, but not synchronously.

To my questions about his state of mind or feeling he would merely giggle or twitch, and he responded similarly to his friends' questions of whether he would like to stay in the hospital. To my question "What do you want to do?" he replied "Take acid with Ralph Metzner." Another staff member questioned him but could elicit no direct responses. When this staff member then turned to the patient's friends and asked "How long has he not been communicating?" there was an immediate response from the patient who exclaimed indignantly, "Communicating!" but further contact was lost immediately.

Later I walked with the patient and his friends to the coffee shop. Mostly he was babbling incoherently, looking around, rolling his eyes. At one point he suddenly placed his hands on the table at which we were sitting, looked straight at us and said in a normal voice, "It's coming in so fast, I can't function at that speed." Contact was made and then he would "go off" again immediately. One had the impression of someone on a high-speed rollercoaster who every now and then could land, make a quick statement to bystanders and then was swept off again by uncontrollable energies.

The admitting physician was unable to persuade him to sign voluntary admission papers. He did not refuse; he just wasn't there. He was talking about Buddha, evolution, cosmic energy, etc. One of his friends tried to persuade him to sign the papers by pointing out: "If you sign, you can split anytime you want to." The response was "I've got to figure out the difference between splitting and fusion." On the recommendation of the physician he was finally put on a seventy-two-hour hold by the sheriff's office, pending a court hearing. He was put through the routine questioning procedure—name, age, etc.—for the third time that day. Again, inconsequential answers, except to "What state were you born in?"—to which the response came lightning fast: "state of innocence." That evening and the next morning he refused food and medication, but was otherwise quiet and peaceful.

The day after his admission to the hospital, I asked Tom if he wanted to try the sensory deprivation or meditation chamber. After I explained the setup he agreed to try it. Getting to the room on the next floor took quite a long time since he would stop from time to time and stare for several minutes at, say, a doorknob, a passing person, or some trees outside the window. He was also talking incoherently, his face twitching and eyes rolling in the manner previously described. Finally Tom lay down in the dark room on the mattress. I explained I would be sitting next door working at a desk, and we could communicate, if desired, via the intercom. After he lay down in the room and I turned off the light and closed the door, I could hear him babbling for a few more minutes and then he fell completely silent. The intercom would have picked up the sound of him turning on the mattress, but there was nothing. I assumed after a while that he must have fallen asleep.

After an hour or so, I opened the door and invited him to come out. He was not asleep but lying perfectly still with his eyes open, staring straight up. He had clearly been awake and silent the whole time. I had to ask him several times to get up and come back to the ward for lunch, before he responded. He said, in a quiet normal voice, "I've been schizophrenisized." As we were walking down the hallway, he said, "The question is whether to stay catatonic." To which I replied, "You could stay catatonic—or not." Later on that day and in the following days he was reported by the staff to be spending long periods of time standing in the bathroom, perfectly still, with his hands clasped in front of his chest.

It was my impression that the dark and quiet room enabled him to control or slow down somewhat the overwhelming flood of sensory information pouring into his senses. He later told me that being in that room helped him to sort out which thoughts were his and which belonged to other people. Humphrey Osmond and others had speculated that unrecognized telepathic receptivity was one of the features contributing to anxiety and confusion in naturally occurring schizophrenia. By eliminating or reducing external sensory input, the dark chamber made this task of sorting and differentiating easier. This would explain why Tom was so much calmer and more self-possessed when he emerged.

It seemed to me that the assumption of an almost motionless posture could also have been an attempt to slow down the torrent of sensory input. When I asked Tom why he was standing like that, he replied, "It seemed the appropriate thing to do after being in the sensory deprivation chamber." He explained the clasping of his two hands and the immobility as an attempt to prevent the two halves of his body image from separating. In other words, what the psychiatrist would diagnose, and in fact later did diagnose, as pathological "waxy flexibility" (*flexibilitas cerea*) could be seen as an intentional posture to cope with excessive stimulation and a fear of "falling apart."

The facial twitching and rolling of the eyes disappeared completely after this first session. He explained the eye movements as him "going into the next room"—in other words, escaping. This comment reminded me of something Wilhelm Reich had written in his book

Character Analysis, when he related how a schizophrenic girl used an upward turning of the eyes to "go off."

Tom's next sensory deprivation and counseling session was terminated after about two hours by a nurse returning him to the ward for lunch. As he emerged from the dark room he said, "I always did want to be an astronaut." The calm induced by the sessions in the room, however, did not survive his return to the ward, where the stimulation caused by his interactions with the other patients and staff would send him back on his somewhat agitated "trip." During the next two weeks we ran two more sensory deprivation sessions, and I talked with Tom almost daily. Although the sessions were voluntary, and Tom could have terminated them at any time, he never did. In fact several times he requested more of them. Staff reports were that he was generally cooperative and quiet on the ward. Although he talked from time to time of his desire to leave, he did not take the necessary steps to be considered for discharge.

About two weeks after admission he was seen walking off the hospital grounds. He was then transferred to a locked ward with mostly elderly chronic schizophrenics. The physician in charge decided that electroconvulsive therapy (ECT) was indicated, although when I objected that this would interfere with my ongoing treatment, it was temporarily deferred. The stated reason for giving ECT was that "acute psychoses tend to develop chronic patterns if not interrupted early in their course, and there is ample evidence that ECT is the treatment of choice, especially since the patient has been uncooperative in taking oral medications." Privately, the resident in charge told me that "the patient was taking too long to come down from his trip."

While Tom was on the locked ward, I was able to persuade him to sign the voluntary admission papers, which cleared the way for voluntary self-discharge. When he was transferred back to the open ward, he irritated the staff there by refusing to take medication, by visiting other wards, and by "fraternizing with female patients." It was also alleged that he and two other patients had smoked marijuana on the grounds. Other "psychotic behavior" that had been observed included lying on the floor, banging his head against the wall, spitting in the drinking fountain, and talking threateningly to other patients. These behaviors were considered sufficient reason for giving ECT after all.

During the period these behaviors were observed by the ward staff, my talks with Tom continued, and he was in excellent contact. I pointed out to him the likely consequences of his aggressive behavior, and he appeared to understand this. One of the attending physicians also described him as having "exquisitely acute contact." It appeared that his state of consciousness fluctuated wildly from day to day and even hour to hour, from total catatonic withdrawal to sharp, immediate here-now awareness. My efforts at this time were directed at getting him to center himself and to balance the wild swings. His ability to "snap out of" the catatonic postures when his interest was aroused indicated to me that the postures were still semivoluntary attempts to achieve inner calm by outer immobility. Some of his talk was about Zen, which advocates a still posture as a way of quieting the mind.

After the first ECT, further treatments were discontinued because Tom's attorney intervened, stating she was obtaining a writ to prevent these treatments. Tom's behavior on the ward began to take on more religious overtones. On two or three occasions he was observed praying in a kneeling position. He also started complaining about the food and telling other patients and staff they should stop smoking. When I pointed out to him that, although I agreed smoking was hazardous, he should work on his own problems and not interfere with others, he replied, "But they're all me." On that very same day I had to ironically take note of a newspaper statement by a Stanford University Nobel Prize–winning chemist that smoking was not only hazardous to the smoker but also to others close enough to breathe the smoke. Many of the staff and physicians at this time were still habitual smokers.

A few days later another incident occurred that led to the resumption of ECTs. At seven o'clock in the morning Tom was seen kneeling in the hallway, apparently praying. When one of the technicians asked him what he was doing, he replied, "Watch your language, soul and spirit." Then he rose up on his knees, spread his arms, "made strange noises," and fell back on the floor. It was clear that the technician and some of the other patients were scared, although no one was actually hurt or hit. Three ECTs were given over the next three days.

Following this series of treatments there was a marked change in Tom's behavior. He seemed to have "come down" from his trip. He was able to talk coherently with staff and other patients. He was regarded by everyone as being more "in contact." However, privately he complained to me that he felt worse. He stated that he was confused, that he no longer remembered things, that the ECTs were harming him, and that he felt irritable and anxious. This was in contrast to his state before the ECT when he felt free and had been able to "see things" and "see through people." When I pointed out to him that he was so out of contact that he did not perceive how he was frightening and threatening other patients and staff, he seemed genuinely surprised. During the next few days he improved consistently in outward behavior but continued to maintain that he was very dissatisfied and unhappy. A week later he was discharged.

The ECT seemed to have effectively interrupted his psychotic episode. The textbook rationale for administering ECT was to prevent an acute psychotic episode from "consolidating" into a chronic state. The convulsions are thought to "shake up" incipient paranoid structures. In an alternative view of psychosis, such as that proposed by Gregory Bateson, R. D. Laing, and others, the psychotic regression is only a temporary phase of a total self-healing process, a circular journey backward in time in order then to move forward again. The meaning of madness, in this view, is that it is a temporary disintegration of psychic structures which, if supported and protected, then allows the innate regenerative processes of the psyche to reestablish equilibrium.

Whether or not one accepts such a model for psychoses in general, it certainly seems applicable to a psychotic episode induced or triggered by mind-altering drugs. The crucial difference here is that the individual usually remembers that he took a drug that changed his consciousness and knows from prior experience and observations that drug trips are temporary alterations of consciousness. The importance of this remembered knowledge and the difference from non-drug-induced psychotic episodes cannot be overemphasized.

The individual on such a trip has a drive to understand and to figure things out. There is acceptance and even occasional enjoyment of "weird" or unusual perceptual phenomena, as well as flashes of real insight and heightened philosophical understandings, all of which is mixed with obvious distress. The reduced ability to control one's perceptual and mental processes interferes with the "normal" learned patterns of interpersonal communication. In effect, such a person may be thinking and even saying, "How can you expect me to carry my tray, when I'm figuring out how God created matter?" There was often exquisite insight and poignancy to Tom's comments.

The sessions in the sensory deprivation chamber or quiet room definitely did provide the individual with a very convincing experience of reduced flooding by sensory stimuli. As Tom's changed behavior and comments after emerging from the chamber showed, he was able to adjust his behavior to meet the "normal" expectations of those around him. Unfortunately, the situation of the quiet chamber in the midst of a state hospital for mental illness could not provide the institutional and staff support for an ongoing healing process with the flood of heightened inner and outer sense stimuli.

Follow-Up: Thirty-Six Years Later

I lost touch with Tom completely over the next years, until unexpectedly, in 2004, I received an e-mail from him reminding me of our meeting at Mendocino State Hospital in 1968. He had looked me up after seeing a video about Tim Leary in which I appeared. He said he was doing well, had his own business in computer programming and Web design, and was playing music with a jazz band and two singer-songwriters. He mentioned that he had explored a number of different consciousness-expansion programs, including Silva Mind Control, Transcendental Meditation, biofeedback, neurolinguistic programming, hypnosis, Arica training, the est training, and some shamanic training with the Harner method. He also wrote, "I spent a couple of years sitting with a Zen group once a week and, after 9/11, I stopped sitting and took up swing dancing. Now I've stopped that and am back to playing music, which I've done since I was eight."

In his e-mail, he described being "rather spaced out" when he was brought to Mendocino State Hospital from Haight-Ashbury in 1968. He wrote the following:

I remember a therapist raising my hand. Of course, because she was a therapist, I left it in the air. I remember she then pointed at me, laughed, and said "he's catatonic." I remember lying on a mattress on the floor in a darkened room wearing headphones. I remember taking a trip to the moon in my mind and you talking to me through the headphones. [The first manned moon landing, Apollo 11, had occurred in 1969.—RM] I remember going outdoors with you. I thought I was in the Garden of Eden, and you led me out of the garden.

I remember lying in the hospital room and wiggling my feet to get through time tunnels to London and you telling me not to talk about that. I remember getting three electroshock "treatments." I remember four big guys holding me down on a table and someone giving me a shot. I remember my lawyer got the electroshocks stopped. I remember going to court to testify that I was sane and being released. Later that year I also spent some time at Napa State Hospital. All of this started because I was sitting on the sidewalk in San Francisco outside a gift store that sold Buddhist items, including a statue of Buddha. I was meditating. A policeman picked me up and took me to San Francisco General Hospital where they gave me Thorazine. Since then, my story about that is that in India I would have been revered as a saint. I was never allowed to finish that meditation to its ultimate depth.

I was naturally pleased to receive Tom's e-mail after so many years of no contact or follow-up connection. I e-mailed him back with appreciation and told him that I had written up his "case" for a psychiatric journal back in 1969 and offered to send him a copy of the article, if he wished. I was somewhat apprehensive about how he would react to the psychiatric jargon I knew I had to use to get the article published. In my e-mail I added:

Just remember that it's written, like all such reports, in the technical language required by the journals. I felt it was my responsibility to alert the psychiatric establishment to the fact that there were other approaches to psychosis, especially trips with LSD, than the usual ones of drugs or shock. I had a supportive chief of psychology, and at first the psychiatrists in charge of your treatment were intrigued by what I, with you, was trying to accomplish with the sensory deprivation chamber. Then you started acting a little bit more weird and they freaked and decided to give you ECT. I argued with them vehemently in several staff meetings, pleading with them to give my approach more time. But I was outgunned by the MDs. I was very upset and pissed off. I'm glad to hear you're doing well and still involved in expanding your consciousness.

Tom wrote back, saying he was interested in seeing the article "about my experiences during that time in 1968 from your point of view. . . . Perhaps reading the article will trigger more memories. I think I would like to use a pseudonym if I can contribute anything to a republishing of the article." He also wrote that he had considered contacting his former psychiatrist and suing the hospital for giving him ECT, saying that he had had

a tightness in the right temple since 1968 and much of my experiments with mind and body have been in an effort to get rid of the tightness, which sometimes becomes painful. I really don't know that ECT was the cause. It may have been an impacted upper right wisdom tooth that was extracted that year. It may have been because I heard Pete Seeger ask in one of his songs, "Why do the kids put beans in their ears?" and I put a bean in my right ear to find out why. I went to a hospital to have it taken out. They poured

*oil in my ear and used tweezers to remove the bean but it hurt when
it was removed.*

*Over the past year I have had the sensation that my skull is
physically too small for my brain. It feels tight. Psychologically, I feel
there is an area of my mind that I can't get to, that is blocked from
me. I'm pretty sure that marijuana or psychedelics would allow me
to access it . . . but I do not consider their use to be options for me at
this time. And so I continue to try all these other paths.*

*I've also in the past year and a half tried to get a medical diagnosis,
but the good news and the bad news is that all tests come up negative:
MRI, MRA, CAT scan, blood tests, neurologist, dentist, etc. I've
been to two physical therapists who couldn't help me: one who does
craniosacral work said my sphenoid bone is stuck and an osteopathic
manipulation doctor who also said my skull bones are stuck. I went to
a biofeedback trainer and after talking with her for two hours she said
she was really stuck and couldn't help me. I tried hypnotherapy and
couldn't access that area of my head, the tightness in the right temple.*

Four or five days after sending Tom a copy of my article from the
psychiatric journal I received an eight-page, single-spaced response
from him. It was basically an angry and articulate denunciation of the
psychiatric and psychological professions and their shortcomings as
currently practiced. I found myself in basic agreement with much of
the criticism, while also reluctantly aware of the systemic difficulties
that stand in the way of a more humane approach to mental illness.
Below are some extracts from Tom's critique, with some comments of
mine interspersed in brackets.

*My first reaction on reading the phrase "LSD psychosis" in the title
was one of anger. I did not then in 1968 and do not now in January*

2005 perceive myself to have been in a state of psychosis. I resent that my state was labeled as such. . . . Dr. Metzner had warned me . . . nevertheless I feel critical of the pejorative way of labeling people in the fields of psychiatry and psychology.

My view is that I was not having a schizophrenic experience. I was having an integrative experience. We normally live in a state of schizophrenia (reference to work of R. D. Laing, The Politics of Experience*). The electroshocks that I received prevented me from "digesting" the experience I was having and integrating it into my previous and ongoing experience. I have spent the past thirty-six years searching for ways to reaccess the experience so that I can recover the information from it and integrate the experience into my life.*

The electroshocks have done me irreparable damage, functionally, psychologically, and affectively if not physiologically, and in their ignorance and pathetic narrow-mindedness the individuals responsible for recommending and implementing them have done me and society a great disservice. Electroshocks are a cruel and barbaric practice, a form of brutal assault and battery that attempts to coerce an individual to conform to the pitiful limitations of socially approved states of consciousness [reference to work of Peter Breggin, Toxic Psychiatry*].*

Our cultural proclivities toward having a pejorative view of experiences different from our own normally limited states of consciousness caused my state to be labeled "psychosis," "schizophrenia," and "catatonia." My own view of my state, which I continue to assert, is that had I been in India, I would have been revered as a saint who was meditating in a high state of realization. [This view, which was current in some circles in the 1960s, is incorrect. Indian society, which is highly stratified along religious and caste lines, has a number of different ways of categorizing and explaining what the West calls "mental illness," but they are quite clear about the difference between psychotic, confused states and states of high spiritual realization. —RM]

In my paper, I had written about "the theoretical feasibility but practical difficulty of allowing the psychotic to go on his trip and the necessity of considering the whole ecological framework in which this kind of work is done." Tom reacted to this statement by saying,

What I needed at the time was hugs, caring, and understanding, not electroshocks. Hugs in particular would have been of immense help to me. Had I been allowed to complete the experience on my own, with loving support, I would have integrated it into my life and moved on. . . . One should provide a person experiencing states of consciousness different from the norm with rooms in a nice house, with a garden, pleasant and comfortable surroundings.

He went on to quote with approval the work and attitude of Patch Adams and the Gesundheit! Institute. Again, I was in total agreement with the desirability of such an approach for the poor souls lost on their inner journeys—while recognizing the difficulty of integrating such methods into a state mental health facility.

Tom criticized inaccuracies I had in my secondhand descriptions of his life prior to the hospitalization and seemingly took offense at what I had reported about life in the Haight-Ashbury commune. He wrote:

So because my interests were different from those of my friends they considered me a burden. If I was not contacting them, why

didn't they contact me? Physical contact, i.e., hugging and massage, would have helped establish contact and ameliorated the anxiety and confusion. [He seemed to be unable to see, even decades later, how his behavior was distancing and confusing to those around him who cared for him. —RM]

In reaction to reading my descriptions of his facial expressions and mannerisms at the time of intake to the hospital, Tom wrote:

Whatever the case, I was intensely involved in my internal mental experience. Geniuses throughout history have had experiences of going for days or weeks without communicating with others due to their intense involvement in internal states. . . . The fact that I answered some questions immediately and clearly while ignoring others showed that I responded to those subjects in which I was interested and ignored those in which I was not interested. What a tragedy that my integrity was not respected by those around me. As I read the descriptions of my behavior and what I said, I am proud of the internal research I was doing at the time and what I said in response to questions. I knew exactly what I was doing and I reaffirm and stand by my efforts. What a remarkable and heroic experience.

In my book *Allies for Awakening* I wrote about the problem of over-idealization and grandiosity that can occur with loosely structured psychedelic explorations, such as those that were common in the 1960s. In our community life in Millbrook, New York, which was oriented around the creative and constructive use of psychedelics, we would all too often experience someone reappearing in the community from the retreat cabin with a wild-eyed stare that said, "I've found the deepest secret of the universe and need to share it, so people will recognize me for its profound significance." We would then ruefully roll our eyes and ask someone to keep an eye on the "lost in space" explorer to make sure he or she stayed physically safe. Clearly, Tom had exceeded his community's capacity to protect his safety and well-being—and he was grandiosely unaware of and unconcerned with the burden he was imposing on others. The thoughts and visions he was having—some of them profound, some less so—were too important for him to be concerned with the social niceties.

In his second, longer letter, Tom wrote that

> *sensory deprivation was not a good choice of treatment. This process increased my involvement with my internal mental processes and exacerbated my disconnect with my body, my sensory experience, and external physical reality . . . it made me schizophrenic and catatonic and was the opposite of what I needed. . . . A more effective method for encouraging me to connect with bodily sensations, sensory experience, other people, and external physical reality in a more normally functional way would have been to hug and massage my body.*

For me, as the psychologist who provided Tom and the hospital with the quiet room, the sensory deprivation chamber, this statement disavowing any benefit from it came as somewhat of a shock. In his initial letter to me, quoted above, he had said of his experience in the dark room: "I remember taking a trip to the moon in my mind and you talking to me through the headphones. I remember going outdoors with you. I thought I was in the Garden of Eden and you led me out of the garden." As I noted above, he was very quiet while in the dark space, and afterward for a while, and then gradually the overstimulation of the general ward seemed to disrupt his behavior.

So here we have a mystery or a paradox—at least to this psychologist's eyes. My observations at the time and Tom's own behavior confirmed that his stays in the quiet, dark room stabilized his swings of mood and erratic confused verbalizations—at least temporarily. In his account written thirty years later, he denies it had any beneficial effect; in fact, he says it did the opposite. To my statement that "the calm induced by the sessions in the dark room usually did not survive the return to the ward" Tom wrote:

Of course not! The psychiatric ward of a state mental hospital is a chaotic environment. Nobody in their right mind would want to be there. People in this situation, as I was, are very sensitive to their surroundings and to the behavior and states of mind of others. As is widely known with the use of entheogens, setting is an important factor in the experience that a person has using them.

So this is perhaps the answer to the paradox: While the calm mood in the quiet room was real—enabling an imaginary ride to the moon and a walk in the Garden of Eden—it was cut short immediately on return to the ward. The inner/outer chaos returned, along with indignation at the cold and insensitive treatment by the regular hospital staff and environment. In conclusion, Tom wrote:

My view of the meaning of the experiences I had in 1968 is radically different from the psychiatric view. Psychiatry did me harm and injury in several ways and I have spent thousands of

dollars attempting to undo the harm. I have explored nondrug
means of regaining my wholeness. So far, I have not been able to
recover that which I lost in 1968 and which is still blocked from
my consciousness and inaccessible to me.

For my part, what I realized from rereading my original report together with Tom's subsequent elaborations of his chaotic inner world at the time is that I overestimated his familiarity with mind-expanding experiences with drugs such as LSD. He was apparently a relatively inexperienced tripper in those sometimes chaotic settings and times. In his letter he had written that in 1967, in a Los Angeles-area commune, he "took LSD (purple heart, 200 mcg) for the first time with about one hundred people who were living there." Hardly an ideal supportive environment.

I do not know how many other drug trips he had, but it was only about a month later that his strange behavior while living in the San Francisco area led to his being brought to the state hospital. Later on in the '60s and '70s, the underground culture did become more skillful at helping people navigate through difficult trips. Reminding someone lost in space that they had taken a drug with an effect that would wear off with time became accepted, standard practice in the hippie underground. These were the early years.

More experienced trippers develop navigational skills, such as meditation and concentration, with which they learn to find their way through difficult states and help others do the same. At the time, I was beginning to actively practice and teach such skills, but Tom had no experience with them. In retrospect it might have been more helpful to both of us if I had somehow been able to engage him more in describing his experience and trying to understand it on his own terms. He might have felt more encouraged—even without the massage that he wanted so badly. I was also feeling the pressure from the psychiatrists at the hospital to prove that one could help people go through these confused psychosis-like states induced by psychedelics without drastic, potentially damaging interventions such as ECT.

◆ ◆ ◆

In conclusion, I present here a list of the differences and partially overlapping features of psychotic states and psychedelic states of consciousness, especially when the latter occur in a supportive setting.

1. *Dissolution of perceived boundaries between self and world:* perceived with panic in psychotic states; with delight and awe in psychedelic states.
2. *Sense of Time:* in psychotic states the sense of time becomes static, slowed down, and unchanging; in psychedelic states, time is transcended into a timeless and expansive state.
3. *Sense of Space:* in psychotic states the sense of space tends to be flat, constricted, narrow, tight; in psychedelic states expanded, with more depth and more fluidity.
4. *Feeling State:* the feeling state in psychosis tends to be depressed, anxious, angry; with psychedelics, delighted, euphoric, humorous.
5. *Sensory Experience:* psychotic states tend to be cut-off from body sensations, focused on abstract, often paranoid thought processes; in psychedelic states there is less interest in abstract ideas, more interest in subtle sensory experience.
6. *Perception of Reality:* in psychotic states, reality is perceived

and received as is—with no awareness of the difference between one's subjective experience and objective reality; in psychedelic states there is simultaneous perception of the objective outer reality and one's own multifaceted subjective experience—the difference is recognized and simultaneously transcended.

2

Guidance on Intimacy Received from the Goddess Artemis

Carl, a successful physician, consulted me for guidance on his problems with intimacy. He would become friends and then become intimate with a succession of women, but then after a couple of months of being together, would find himself withdrawing. He still liked the woman—they shared many interests—but he did not want to become engaged or married. Experiencing considerable pressure from his Mormon family to get married, he was distressed at his own apparent fear of committing to a long-term relationship.

The major trauma of Carl's childhood was that his father committed suicide and his mother died in an accident a year later. He was raised by his grandparents. Years of psychotherapy had helped him come to a place of peace about the loss of his parents but had not affected his fear of intimacy.

By way of preparation for our intensive session, I introduced Carl to the practice of what I call the Medicine Wheel of Spirit

Guides or Four Gateways of Being. A cross with equal-length arms inside a circle or wheel is one of the most ancient symbols and practices of meditation and integration. C. G. Jung and his followers wrote extensively about the mandala, a wheel and cross symbol of individuation adopted from the Indian tantra system that, when it appears in dreams, often presages an integrative process. Jung observed that as his patients progressed in their individuation process, they would tend to dream and draw more mandala-like images. The notion of "four shields" in the Native American tradition is a similar cluster of symbols and images associated with the four directions, the four seasons, and many other quaternities. Symbolic depictions of the four shields are used in initiation ceremonies, as well as individual practices. The use of the word *shield* implies that the fourfold figure functions as protection against distractions and intrusions from outside, as well as a focus for concentration on inner processes.

Steven Foster and Meredith Little, with whom I shared many wonderful wilderness experiences and stories, wrote a treatise on this subject called *The Four Shields*, based on their studies of Native American cultures and initiation ceremonies. They write:

> The four seasons, faces, personas, shields of human self thus correspond to and consist of the four seasons, faces, personas— shields of the earth. In humans, the four faces are: summer (the emotional, instinctive, physical, reactive, body-child), fall (the inward, self-conscious, psychological soul of transition), winter (the rational, responsible, controlled, interdependent mind of maturity) and spring (the regenerating, healing, creative spirit of that which is born from death). Body, psyche, mind and spirit. (Foster and Little 1999, 4)

The countless variations in the medicine wheel symbolism include the particular animals, environmental elements, colors, qualities, and teachings that are associated with each of the four directions. It's not as if there is only one correct version. I lean toward an ecological and geographical perspective. For those living on the East Coast of North America, the Atlantic Ocean is clearly the dominant presence, whereas for West Coast dwellers, the Pacific Ocean dominates the landscape. Universally, east is associated with morning and sunrise, west with evening and sunset. For those living in the northern hemisphere, a northern direction leads to cold, dark, and winter, a southern direction to warmth, light, and summer. But go below the equator to South Africa, South America, and Australia and the associated seasonal qualities change again, from the tropical north to the frigid Antarctic south.

The following version of the Medicine Wheel is rooted in the geography and ecology of the west coast of North America, where the sun sets on the magnificent Pacific Ocean, and going southward we come to the tropical lands with their sun-drenched ecosystems. The ecological qualities of each geographical direction are metaphorically correlated with the four core archetypes of youth and old age, male and female.

There are an infinite number of ways to divide the cosmos of our life-world into a quaternity or fourfold mandala, no one more correct than another. Each one has its virtues. The associations of the seasons, the life cycle, and directions in Foster and Little's *Four Shields* are different from the ones described here. They also describe different shields for men and women. The medicine wheel I have used is based on the view that our basic nature is androgynous. Each of us is both masculine and feminine in our essence and expression, regardless of the vast and wonderful spectrum of differences between men and women. A core aspect of the path toward wholeness is balancing the polarity of male and female within each one of us, regardless of the gender of our outer form. The second core polarity in which we are all inescapably involved is that of youth and old age. These are the Four Gateways of Being.

~

The Medicine Wheel of Spirit Guides or Four Gateways of Being

To prepare for the practice you are invited to invoke your spirit allies and guides—the inner helpers and teachers that are already known to you. If you are doing this kind of practice for the first time, you can simply invoke your Higher Self or Inner Guide Self—however you conceive it. We are going to connect with four great archetypes that represent personifications of your own intuitive Guiding Self. In practice, you will be attending and focusing on one of these figures at a time. The divination consists of posing a question and receiving an answer. Visualize your personal shield of lighted awareness in the whole chest area, with light and purifying fire radiating out in all directions. This shield of light and fire encompasses not only the heart chakra in the middle of the chest but the whole large, warm, and embracing spherical space encompassed by the rib cage and the shoulders down to the upper abdomen.

For a divination practice it is best to choose one question and ask that same question at each of the four gateways of the Medicine Wheel of Spirit Guides. Your question could concern (1) personal problem solving, (2) guidance for the future, (3) family or community problem solving, or (4) the collective planetary future. In addition to a question, you may also choose to ask each of the four Archetypal Beings in the four directions for a symbolic gift—and they may indeed choose to give you an object or show you something, rather than give a verbal answer. Their response to your question may be a feeling, a flash of intuition, or a subtle change of mood. You should stay centered in the heart-center space throughout, with the attitude of a compassionate witness or empathic observer. After each of the four question-and-answer exchanges, be sure to acknowledge with gratitude the answer received—even if you do not fully understand it. It is also helpful for you to verbalize out loud whatever answer you receive to your divination question. Allow a few moments of rest and quiet contemplation after each question-and-answer exchange.

Go to the Eastern Gateway—
The Place of Sunrise

Tuning in to this archetype may be facilitated by remembering a peak ecstatic experience of your childhood. Ask to connect with the Inner Wise Child, the Golden Child, or the Divine Youth or Maiden. Or you may choose to invoke a child-god figure such as the Child Krishna or Child Jesus. You can ask for a name or other descriptive identifier for this Being. Even if you don't receive an answer, it doesn't hurt to ask, and it will facilitate tuning in during other divinations. Ask your preselected divination question—and wait a moment in a receptive mode. Note the answer you receive, whether it's in words, symbols, or other gifts. You may ask for further clarification. In closing, acknowledge the answer received and give thanks.

Go to the Southern Gateway—
The Place of the Garden Goddess

Ask to connect with a female spirit guide or deity that represents your feminine soul or anima, or a mythic goddess to whom you feel connected, such as Shakti, Mary, Isis, or Quan Yin. If you don't recognize the figure from previous encounters, you could ask for her name. If you don't get a name, note any distinctive feature, like the color of her robe or her hair, any object she holds, or an animal that accompanies her. Ask your divination question and receive and note the answer, whether in words or symbols. Instead of a verbal response the figure may simply give you a gift or make a gesture. Note any specific shapes or colors—afterward you may want to look up these specifics in a guide to mythic goddesses. You may also choose to draw or paint the figure that you see. You may ask for further clarification on the answer you received. Acknowledge the answer or vision and give thanks to the Garden Goddess.

Go to the Northern Gateway—
The Place of the Mountain God

Ask to connect with your masculine soul, the animus, male spirit guide, or a deity, such as Shiva, Hermes, Osiris, or Kokopelli. If you don't recognize the figure, you can ask for a name. Note any specific identifiers like color of skin, clothing, or hair color, staff or other held object, accompanying animal, etc. Sometimes people report that the figure doesn't seem to have a name, or want to give a name, or says the name is not important. You can say/think inwardly that the point of having a name is that it facilitates getting in touch with that being in the future—it's your "access code" to that deity. It's like exchanging phone numbers or e-mail addresses when you meet a new friend. Ask your divination question of the Mountain God and note the answer received, whether it's direct or symbolic. Acknowledge and give thanks to that god. We have found that people have much greater difficulty connecting to a "god" because of the heavy load of religious associations to the idea of *God* in Western culture. Remember that the collective mythic consciousness of humanity is peopled with numerous gods and goddesses with whom you can communicate—and doing so does not invalidate your commitment to any figure that you have chosen to be your "one god."

Go to the Western Gateway—
The Place of Sunset

Find yourself at the shore of the ocean in the West, as the sun sinks below the horizon. Ask to connect with your Elder Spirit Guide or Wise Old One, which may be a pair of male and female ancestors. You may connect with the crone aspect of the Triple Goddess or the old-man aspect of the Threefold Hermes. Here too you can ask for a name or note other identifiers, such as the color of clothing, any object held, or an accompanying animal. Pose your divination question again and, after a brief attentive pause, note the answer received. You can repeat the answer

given to confirm it—like saying "you're telling me this . . ."
Give thanks to the Old Ones and return to your here-now
divination starting point. Reflect on the four answers or
responses you received to your question and consciously
allow the meaning to be gradually absorbed into your heart
field.

∿

Sometimes when people go through this divination they report
that they got in touch with a family member or acquaintance—say,
their grandmother as the wise elder or their admired college professor
as a male or female guide. When this happens, I usually recommend
that they look and ask further for the archetypal figure behind and
beyond that individual, the archetype that the particular individual
embodied. Sometimes this maneuver can explain why that particular
individual had such a profound impact on one's life.

Carl's Divination with the
Four Spirit Guides

After the preparatory practices and once he had entered into a mildly
enhanced meditative state of consciousness, I suggested to Carl that
he ask each of these guides the following questions: What can you
tell me about my fear of intimacy? What is its origin and what can I
do about it? We spent about five to ten minutes dialoguing with each
of the four archetypal figures. I would verbalize invoking the figure
and addressing the question, and after tuning in, he would verbalize
the answer he received. His *inner child,* seemingly in a jovial mood
and yet with unmistakable maturity, simply replied, "Relax and don't
worry. You'll get over the fear of intimacy, with time."

His female *anima spirit* replied calmly: "I neither want nor need the kind of long-term intimate relationship you're concerned about." I then suggested to Carl that he ask this anima figure what she does want or need in a relationship. The reply was startling to both of us, but definite: "Nothing, I don't need an intimate ongoing relationship." Both Carl and I then simultaneously realized that his mythic anima spirit was Artemis, the autonomous goddess of the hunt, of healing, of midwifery and childcare, who does not have an ongoing male partner in Greek mythology. As a physician, it felt natural for Carl to be connected with this goddess, and his resonance with her was also expressed in his love of outdoor sports, the mountains, and nature in general.

Carl described his male *animus spirit* as being like the Egyptian Horus deity—a figure accompanied by a "hawk with three eyes." This being, representing Carl's masculine psyche, replied to the question equally calmly: "I'm not afraid of intimacy; I don't have that problem." From this hawk deity spirit, Carl received encouragement that he could and should have the kind of relationship he wanted to have and that he should not be overly concerned with meeting familial expectations that were foreign to his essential nature.

In his conversation with the *inner elders* couple Carl realized that his obsessive drive to find a woman to marry came really more from his Mormon family than from his own inner need or wish. Eventually, at a time and circumstance of his own choosing, he did find and marry a woman that he liked. I do not know whether and how the Artemis archetype expressed itself further in their relationship and their family.

3

Vicissitudes of the Soul on the Journey to a Human Birth

The loss of a child before birth due to an unexpected miscarriage is certainly a cause of deep grief for the parents—as heartbreaking as losing a child to death after birth. The only small comfort in such situations is that, like other medical mishaps, the loss of life is the result of biological forces beyond our control.

A different and often highly charged situation arises when the parents decide to have an abortion. In my experience with hundreds of individuals in my workshops over the years I would estimate that one in four individuals or their parents had experienced an abortion in their lives. Many individuals in my groups related that though they had ultimately come to terms with the intentional termination of a pregnancy, there were often painful aftereffects that could linger for years. Almost always in those situations, one or both parents carry some degree of regret and guilt over the intentional termination of a life—even when there was agreement between the partners and there were morally or medically sound reasons to terminate the pregnancy. One cannot help but feel that the deliberate termination of a life is somehow akin to murder. It goes without saying that the vociferous and sometimes vicious language used by some self-styled "abortion foes" to harass and vilify women seeking the procedure and the providers offering it only adds to the guilt and pain the regretful mothers and their partners already feel about their situation.

One of the *alchemical divination* processes involves having a healing conversation with the soul of a child whose fetal body form was intentionally not carried to term. The psychospiritual basis for this process is the certain knowledge that the soul is immortal and cannot be killed, either before or after birth. Even when the soul of a loved one is disconnected from the body form in which it has chosen to incarnate, whether in death, in sleep, or in deeply dissociated states, the possibility of communion and communication with those still in conscious waking life remains. At the soul level, each of us can communicate with other souls, particularly those souls with whom we relate as family. We can learn and practice bringing this soul communion down to the waking-state personality level, and we can draw on the deep healing wisdom that the soul carries. I will first describe the divination process, which could be done with or without entheogenic amplification, and then relate an example of how it was employed.

~

Divination for Healing Relations
with an Unborn Soul

Center your awareness, your empathy, and your sense of identity in the Cave of the Heart, which is in the area between the shoulders/upper arms and the upper abdomen.

Breathing deeply, invoke the central vertical axis, with a four-armed cross of light at the three centers in this Cave of the Heart: the center for will and courage at the thymus gland between the shoulders; the heart center of healing love relations in the middle of the chest; and the center of nerve-sense perception and communication at the solar plexus in the upper abdomen.

Invoke your healing and guiding spirits—by name if they are known to you from previous spiritual healing work or otherwise just asking for their presence and assistance. Invoke the immortal souls of all of your family relatives—your parents, aunts and uncles, grandparents, siblings, married and beloved partners, children, and grandchildren. All are involved in the birth or death of a child. It does not matter if any of these family members are still alive "in form" or not—we are connecting at the soul level, beyond form. It helps to actually verbalize outwardly the name of the person, not just the familial appellation you called them in the family. Doing the invocation this way helps to confirm the relations between the souls, which are deeper, more mature, and wiser than the personal familial relations. Thus, we don't say "Mom" or "Grandpa," as we called them in childhood, we say "Mother Anne" or "Grandfather Norman." We have found, in our ceremonies, that people were often moved and delighted how this simple linguistic maneuver facilitates tuning in with a person's essence, not just their family relationship label.

You, the person doing the invocation, are primarily invoking your ancestors and family members—but of course also your partner or ex-partner involved with the aborted child. It is a matter of choice and circumstance as to what extent the absent partner's family web may also be invoked. Matters of life and death always involve and affect the whole family, regardless of how much or how little the family members may know or have known of the conceptions and potential births involved. Often in my practice I have observed that when there are miscarriages or abortions in a family, the other living siblings of that unborn child were deeply affected—even when they were told nothing or little of it at the time. So in this healing ritual we intentionally invite all the familial souls to participate.

The core of the familial and ancestral council of souls is the triad of mother, father, and conceived-but-unborn child. Lines of light and empathic communion connect all three souls with each other. If there is another person involved—a therapist or guide leading the divination—then the four individuals make a kind of cross of light and awareness. It is important to remember that the soul of a child is not an immature child but a soul equal in wisdom and understanding to the souls of the parents. The three souls made an agreement to be a family in the world. At the personal level this turned out to be an agreement the personalities involved were unable to keep or chose not to keep. We always have free will to follow our soul's guidance or not.

From the consciousness of this three- or fourfold communion of souls you and the guide can inwardly ask the following questions and receive the answers, which you may have already gathered via intuition.

- Ask to know whether the unborn child was a boy or a girl.
- Ask to know the child's name. Or give the child the name it would have received if it had been born and raised. With

the naming you are introducing this family member to your present and any future family councils—just as you would have if the child had been born.

- Ask the soul of your unborn child whether it is holding any negativity or judgment toward you the parent. It's been my experience that while parents often have much guilt over the loss of life in an abortion and even with a spontaneous miscarriage, in the communication exchanges with the souls involved there has never been any accusation or negativity from the unborn child's soul. The telepathic and empathic message invariably received and shared is: "Souls can't be killed. I'm not dead. We can communicate. Don't blame yourself."

- You can also ask the unborn soul if there is any further message it wants to convey to you.

There are two additional divination questions that one can ask when in communion with the soul of the unborn. Not everyone is interested in pursuing these questions, but some individuals may be. One is to ask if you and the child soul had a connection in a past life and if so, what your respective roles were in that life. I have found, as have other past-life therapists, that family members often have more than one lifetime of relationship—but often in startlingly different parent-child and even gender roles. Finding such a connection can be quite illuminating when it comes to present-life issues and challenges. A second possible question to ask is whether the soul of your child has incarnated again after the aborted attempt, and if so, whether it is in a family known to you in your present life.

After the series of divination questions, we move on to making a series of empowering and connecting statements, without blame or guilt, addressed to the unborn soul. These can be made inwardly and quietly, but they are more effective if made out loud, *authentically and from the heart*—addressing the unborn child's soul by name. When I work as a therapist guiding someone through this healing process, I say the statement and then ask the person to repeat it.

- "I accept you now as my child, and you may have me as your father/mother."
- "I am sorry that it didn't work out."
- "I am giving you now a place in my heart."
- "You shall participate in the good things that I shall bring about in memory of you."
- "I would like to stay connected with you, as we both wish, in this way."

At the end of the divination ritual, you express your gratitude to the soul of the unborn child, the other parent, and the assembled council of family members and ancestors for participating in this healing and divination family council.

Susan, a woman in her fifties, came to one of my workshops and asked to work with the process called "Healing Relations with the Unborn." She related the following story of an abortion she had undergone as a young woman, with lingering painful aftereffects.

I had been out of MBA school for about a year and was enjoying my first job. At a party I attended with my roommate Cindy I met a darling guy named Chuck. We connected immediately and started dating. He was the first person I had ever fallen in love with; so much so that I fully opened myself to him. Although I was very responsible about birth control and had the most cutting-edge IUD in place, within a couple of months I was pregnant.

During the same week that I found out I was pregnant, I was also promoted to a position that would require monthly travel to New York City. My first trip was to be in two weeks. There was no question in my mind what I had to do. First, my parents would totally freak out if they knew I was pregnant. And second, it would really impact my ability to step up to the responsibilities of my new job. So without considering any other options, I scheduled an abortion at Planned Parenthood. Abortion had only been legal in the United States for a couple of years, and I was a huge proponent of a woman's right to make this choice if she felt this was best for her. I let Chuck know about the pregnancy and what I was going to do. After recovering from the shock, he was supportive.

The day before Thanksgiving in 1976, Cindy took me to Planned Parenthood to get the abortion. It was a horrible experience! It felt like the life force was being sucked out of me. Afterward, I started having a lot of emotional issues that went untreated. I intuitively knew that the child had been a boy and I kept talking about him. Chuck couldn't handle it and about five months later broke up with me. That made it even worse. It wasn't until I got with the man I married that I began to start processing the pain of this experience out of my system. But even after thirty years, there was still lingering pain, grief, and guilt surrounding this choice I had made. When Ralph said we were going to work

*with healing the aftereffects of abortion, all my systems went on
high alert.*

In preparation for the healing process, we first did a light-fire
meditation focused in the heart center and invoked the ancestors
and guiding spirits of all the people involved. We invoked the triad
consisting of the souls of mother, father, and unborn (aborted) child.
All three members of this sacred triad, along with me as the guide,
formed a cross of light that connected all participants with enlightened awareness and empathy.

I then suggested that Susan ask the aborted child's gender, which
she had already intuited was a boy at the time she was pregnant. I
suggested that, once the contact was made, the parent soul ask the
child soul if it was holding any negativity or judgment about the
abortion, the cutting short of a life before being born. I have guided
and assisted such a process many times and without exception I have
found that the unborn souls do not hold a grudge; they seem to
come from a place that recognizes life in a human body as a temporary embodied phase in the infinite existence of an immortal soul.
Recognizing this truth in the oneness of the three immortal souls
allows the person to forgive themselves at the personality level—a
process that the souls involved, in their beingness beyond time, have
long completed.

In our divination process, I then asked Susan to repeat after me,
either inwardly or out loud, the following statements addressing the
soul of the unborn child: "I accept you now as my child, and you
may have me as your mother. I am sorry that it didn't work out. I
am giving you now and holding for you always a place in my heart."
Bert Hellinger, from whose work in family constellation therapy I
adapted these statements, calls them "statements of empowerment."

They affirm the reality of the soul connection while acknowledging the grief and guilt at the personal level.

Susan wrote me in a letter afterward:

I was about halfway through internally saying these things, weeping all the while, when a young man's voice stopped me. He said, "Hello, my name is Rob. It is okay, Susan. My contract was not with you. I am with Dad." I was overjoyed to have finally connected directly to this being that I had carried inside of me and to know that he was okay. It was very healing and meaningful to me. But I was somewhat confused over his statement. Chuck had kept in touch periodically over the years, and I knew he did not have a child named Rob. So what could this mean? It wasn't until several years later, when he and I were talking, that the truth was revealed. Chuck was sharing with me aspects of his life, telling me about his third wife, Patty, and he mentioned that he was very close to one of her sons. He then said, "His name is Rob." I was floored but had the sense to ask about Rob's age and date of birth. Rob had been conceived by Patty and her first husband two months after I had had my abortion. It wouldn't be until years later that Chuck and Rob would come together to fulfill their father-son contract—whatever that was.

Susan wrote me, and I agreed, that this experience taught a big lesson about how the universe works—how sometimes very slowly and unexpectedly intricate patterns of karma and choice can be worked out. In her life, making this connection enabled Susan to fully release the negative emotional charge and guilt that she had carried around with her for thirty years regarding the abortion she'd had as a young woman. All the souls involved had incorporated their experience into their ongoing life plans and purposes.

4

Longing for the Twin Soul Left Behind in Heaven

Paul consulted me because he had difficulty maintaining an intimate connection in his relationships with women. He would feel, after a certain time, that the woman he was dating was somehow "not the right one," making it difficult for him to commit himself to her. Although there were often common interests and undeniable affection and attraction, he longed to feel a particular affinity with his partner, but this remained elusive.

Paul's birth story was unusual. It turned out that he was the fourth child of professional parents. He had two older sisters and one older brother, but there was a ten-year difference between him and the next older sibling. As a result, his childhood was often lonely as his siblings were all teens with their own interests and both parents were working professionals. In his childhood he played with "imaginary friends." He suffered extreme separation anxiety when he was sent off alone to summer camps.

Since his childhood family situation was unusual, I started our session by asking Paul why his parents decided to have another child ten years after their last previous child—a child that would have no play companions in the family. He told me that after fourteen years of rearing her three older children, his mother had wanted to go back to her professional career. However, somewhat to her surprise and chagrin she became pregnant. In agreement with her husband she decided to abort the child. Two weeks after that abortion, she discovered she was still pregnant—with a twin. After the additional abortion of the twin, Paul's mother was overcome with remorse and intentionally conceived another child, as if to make amends for the aborted twins. This child was Paul.

Cultivating the Attitude of the Empathic Observer

To start our divination and healing work together I guided Paul to enter into a light meditative trance, consciously attending to his breath and invoking the supportive presence of his Higher Self. I coached him in adopting the attitude of an "empathic observer" or "compassionate witness" toward the whole situation and all the individuals involved in it, including himself and, more particularly, his lonely child self. The witness or observer attitude practices balanced perception: one is neither for nor against nor pulling away from anyone, including oneself. The attitude of the observer or witness can, however, become the cold balance of indifference and detachment, the attitude that says "I don't care." We counter that by reaching out with empathy or compassion—giving or offering help when asked for and needed. On the other hand, help offered or given in an overly solicitous way, sympathetically but not wisely, can be ineffective and even counterproductive.

I sometimes use the following vignette to indicate how *empathy* differs from *sympathy*. A man walks down the street and perceives another person who has fallen into a hole in the ground and clearly needs help. Responding instinctively and sympathetically, feeling sorry for the victim and his mishap, the man jumps down into the hole. Now we have two people stuck in the hole. They can console each other and keep each other company, which is certainly better than being stuck alone. Someone with an empathic attitude who comes along sees the man in the hole and says, "I see you are in distress. Let me get a ladder so you can climb out of that hole." This person has enough detachment along with the sympathy to perceive what is needed to solve the problem.

With sympathy you feel as the other person feels—this can be a totally unconscious, unintended reaction, like feeling depressed just by passing a depressed person in the street, without recognizing the connection. With empathy there is, in addition, recognition that you are not that person, though you feel some of the same feelings. Empathy and the authentic expression of it is a key factor in interpersonal conflict resolution. The substance MDMA has been called "empathogenic" for its ability to facilitate or augment empathic interpersonal connection in psychotherapy. The cultivation of compassion or empathy, in conjunction with the balance of wisdom, is also the essential core of Buddhist meditation practice.

As I coached Paul in considering his mother's history with the attitude of the compassionate witness or empathic observer, he could readily understand his mother's overly solicitous nurturance and possessiveness toward him as a child. Overcome with guilt at the initially incomplete abortion of the twins, his mother attempted to compensate by being overly solicitous toward Paul, the child who succeeded in being born. By empathically recognizing his mother's oversolicitousness toward him as her understandable reaction to the unexpected discovery of having aborted twins, Paul was able to let that issue be his mother's to deal with, and no longer resented her for it.

There remained for him the question of how his birth and his fate were connected to that of his twin siblings who died, i.e., were aborted, before he (Paul) was conceived and born. In other words, Paul actually had five older siblings—three who lived and the pair of twins who were aborted before he was born. When I guided him in the practice of merging empathically with all the souls involved in the situation, Paul could recognize that his twin siblings had been conceived but were then aborted because the personalities of the parents did not recognize and did not agree with the agenda of the incoming souls. Souls, being immortal, cannot be aborted or killed—only their physical and personal vehicles or bodies can die or be killed.

I realize that I am making statements here that may carry a strong emotional, religious, or political charge for some readers. I am personally fully in support of a woman's right to determine whether to give birth to a child she is carrying or to terminate the pregnancy if that proves too difficult for whatever reason. Paul and I agreed that in order to disentangle the skeins of his troubled sense of self, we needed to go further back into his complicated prenatal history and connect with the soul wisdom of the individuals involved in a family council. Matters of birth and death always involve the whole family because souls choose the family into which they are born, although the personalities involved, having free will, can choose to agree, ignore, or counter the soul's choices and promptings.

Invocation of a Family Council of Souls

To prepare for the invocation we center ourselves with empathic awareness in the heart-center space of the upper body and expand a spherical field of purifying light-fire energy in all directions. Amplified by mindful breathing, we let the physical, emotional, and mental layers of awareness become infused with the love and wisdom of the immortal soul self and simultaneously connect with the soul selves of all the family members involved in this situation. We thus create a family council of concentric semicircles around the core soul triad of mother, father, and child, or in this case, Paul's mother and father and their six children, those born and the unborn. "Behind" the parents, so to speak, we invoke the souls of grandparents, both maternal and paternal. Sometimes, optionally, one can also invoke the brothers or sisters of the parents (uncles and aunts), especially if they played a significant role in the early family matrix. All of these individuals, their souls and their persons, are involved in matters of birth and death in the family.

It is not necessary to have or create a visual image of the family members making up this council. You invoke them by thinking of them and inviting them, respectfully, as if to a family gathering in ordinary time and space. Nor is it necessary for the core person, in this case Paul, to have ever met or known the individuals personally. Our ancestral lineage carries an important set of preconditions for our existence, and familial karma can be as significant as inherited familial property or debt. We may be connected with family members in sometimes mysterious and unexpected ways.

In my book *Ecology of Consciousness* I relate several true stories of children, and sometimes adults, who remembered, in deep hypnotic memory states or in dreams, making the soul choice to be conceived and then born to a particular set of parents at a particular time. Sometimes a soul may choose to forego birth, either to come in at another, later time or to remain as a soul twin beyond the earthly dimension— accessible in dreams and deep meditative states of union. This is the reasoning and intention behind the divination practice of communing with the core triad of souls—mother, father and child.

I guided and accompanied Paul in a meditative divination, with mild entheogenic amplification, to the family matrix before his conception and birth. He and I both recognized that after the twin souls were blocked from being born by the unexpected double abortion, the incoming twin souls made a second attempt, but this time only one of the twins, a boy, was born; the other one, a girl, stayed behind. Paul recognized that he was the reincarnation of his previously aborted older twin sibling. The soul agreement that the twins made with each other and their parents, in their second attempt to be conceived and born, was that the other twin, a female, stayed behind at the soul level, living in his heart as his beloved anima figure.

In fact, there are strands of esoteric teaching, expressed in certain Gnostic texts, that hold all souls are in a certain sense twins; that when a soul is born, a twin remains behind in the heaven realm and the two are reunited when the earthly twin returns after death.

Perhaps because of the unusual prebirth history in Paul's situation, this memory of the unborn twin soul was particularly vivid.

The recognition of his connection with his beloved unborn twin sister explained to Paul his lifelong desire for a female partner who could match the ideal anima image that he held in his heart of hearts. Recognizing the origin of that longing helped him release the impossible expectation that any other partner could ever match that secret, idealized soul bond.

He understood then that the solution of this dilemma was to magnify the connection to his twin soul, identifying her by name, and connect with her in his own inner meditations. He decided to cease expecting the reincarnation of his beloved twin to manifest in another real woman that he would meet. This, he realized, was an unrealistic expectation and wish that would block him from developing an intimate and fulfilling relationship in the outer real world of family and home.

5

Spider Grandmother Heals the Effects of Childhood Sexual Abuse

During the workshops on alchemical divination and healing that I conducted in Europe during the 1980s and '90s, the participants were introduced to specific divination practices that they could apply to whatever situation presented itself to their awareness. While in group ceremony, there was no talking or question-and-answer process among or from participants, although there were always extended preparatory discussions before and integrative storytelling afterward. With this kind of supportive yet self-disciplined structure, it could sometimes happen that deeply buried traumatic memories unexpectedly came up for healing.

In our workshops we practiced healing meditations based on the teachings of the European alchemical tradition. We also adopted from the shamanic traditions the practice of seeking connection with one or more animal species spirit, referred to variously as "power animal" or "spirit animal," "totem," or "ally." Participants were encouraged to connect with animal spirits with whom they had previously connected and also be open to finding a new animal spirit for whatever healing or visioning project they were anticipating.

In the following story, related by Georgina, a homeopathic practitioner and therapist from Germany, we see how a shamanic spirit ally and a core alchemical operation, both previously unknown to her, played a significant role in helping her heal the residues of childhood sexual abuse and gave her a new spiritual foundation for her work as a healer.

~

Balancing the Dynamic and Receptive Poles of the Energy Field

The energy field, sometimes referred to as the aura, not only surrounds but also interpenetrates the physical body at every level. It can be thought of as a polarized electromagnetic antenna system, both receiving and transmitting energies of diverse vibratory frequencies in the multiple worlds of reality and consciousness. The left side of the human body-and-energy field is the focus of receptive, yin, magnetic, incoming energy flow; the right side is the focus of dynamic, yang, expressive, outgoing energy flow. At the personality levels, these poles correspond in a general way to female and male, but it should be understood that this refers to basic energy polarity, common to men and women, and not to sociocultural images and norms of masculine and feminine.

In the alchemical literature, we find the left-right,

dynamic-receptive polarization consistently symbolized in images of the king standing on the right with the sun beneath his feet and the queen standing on the left with the moon beneath her feet. In the iconography of Indian tantra yoga, a beautiful image symbolic of this polarity is the hermaphroditic Shiva Ardhanarisvara ("two-in-one form")—male on the right side of the body and female on the left side. The balancing and integration of the dynamic and receptive poles of the multidimensional human energy systems into an androgynous wholeness is the central alchemical operation of coniunctio, also called the "inner marriage." The coniunctio is a complex multifaceted process involving many aspects and stages.

We prepare for the practice of the coniunctio operation by invoking the lighted beingness of the Higher Self and letting sensory awareness, with purifying light-fire, spread out from the central axis to the left and right sides, upward and downward, and forward and backward. In this way we amplify our perception of the spherical energy field that interpenetrates the physical body and extends beyond it about fifteen to twenty feet or more in all directions. This spherical energy field, along with the physical and subtle bodies, constitutes what in alchemy is called the "vessel" for the work (opus) of transformation and in shamanism, the "vehicle" for the journey of transformation.

Having established your perception and awareness in the body and energy field—visualized as male on the right and female on the left, both facing forward—you then direct with your intention the right and left halves of the body to turn toward each other, so that the energies and sensations from the two sides flow into and merge with each other. You then observe the changes taking place as this process of merging the left and right poles occurs.

Georgina's response to this process was intense. In her report after the session she wrote that the initial effect was immediate and strong, and she observed her own defensive patterns trying to prescreen her perceptual awareness.

> *As I noted it, I could let go of the defenses and then I became aware of anxiety. I recognized that to me the masculine meant sex and violence. I saw that I was always afraid of men, their sexuality and their violence. I saw various scenes from my childhood, the streets in which I grew up in Hamburg, the red-light district. I saw images of prostitution, sexual violence, and arrogant behavior from men toward women.*
>
> *We were being guided to turn the left and right sides of the bodily energy-field toward each other, as one step of the coniunctio process. Suddenly I became aware of choking-swallowing sensations and simultaneously had the thought that my father had put his penis in my mouth. I was shocked by the appearance of this thought-image and didn't know what to do with it. Up to this point in my life I had never thought that anything like this had happened. At that exact moment I perceived the spider, or rather Spider. She was enormous and situated above me—I was lying under her like under a roof. I knew immediately that she was protecting me, had always protected me, and that she was a deity.*

Georgina then began to converse inwardly with her newly found shamanic ally or power animal, reconstructing step by step how things had gone between her and her father, when she was a little girl around four years old.

> *I was a sweet little coquettish girl. He loved me and was touched by my sex appeal. But he could not express or show his love for me. He had difficulties with feelings anyway. I had no negative feelings whatsoever toward him or toward myself. To see this, and to recognize that it was like that, somehow relieved me. I said—yes, Papa, you did this, you couldn't help yourself.*

Georgina related afterward that she was almost breathless and stunned by these revelations, focusing with full attention and concentration on the dialogue between herself and Spider, who was clearly female. "Ask me questions, ask me questions," she kept repeating while looking directly at Georgina, who perceived her like a "dolled up" old lady, with red lips and small red eyes.

> *I knew then that she was a deity, a very great one, and that she had always been with me. But as a child I had such great fear of her. I had arachnophobia, which I was only able to overcome with psychotherapy.*

I told Georgina about the important and beneficent role Spider plays in the mythology of the Native Americans of the Southwest, of which she was not previously aware. For some tribes, Spider Grandmother is the creator deity who uses her powerful thoughts and dreams to create, guard, and protect the world web in which she lives and everything that exists on Earth. She recreates the web every morning and reabsorbs it every night, just as we do with the threads and webs of our thoughts and images. Here are some passages from the voluminous material on Grandmother Spider on the internet, from many different websites (which contain variations and details). I mention here the elements that I related to Georgina in the healing session.

Grandmother Spider uses Her magical powerful thoughts and dreams to create, guard, and protect everything that exists on Earth and to weave the fabric of time. Her legends are a part of the creation mythology for several southwestern tribes including the Hopi, Pueblo, and Navajo. One myth says that in the beginning of time only two beings were in existence . . . *Tawa* the Sun God, who held all the powers from above, and Grandmother Spider, the Earth Goddess, with all the powers from below. It was Tawa who imagined all of the creatures of Earth and Grandmother Spider who turned these thoughts into living things. It is also believed that she attaches a line of silk to the head of every person she creates so that they will always be connected to her and have access to her wisdom, her teachings, and, if they keep the doorway at the top of their heads open, her protection.

Georgina continued her account of the teachings she received from Grandmother Spider, which turned out to echo many of the Native American beliefs about this deity.

She then revealed to me her competencies and capabilities. She was a master healer, whose poisons could be remedies. I remembered that I was healed by a homeopathic preparation of tarantula, when I had broken my coccyx at the birth of my third son. I somehow intuitively perceived her healing capabilities without being able to express them in words.

Then she gave me a treatment: she crawled on me and tickled me, stung me, and brushed out all my orifices with her hairy legs. Then she went inside me, laid herself on my brain embracing the two hemispheres with her legs, and laid herself on my sternum and embraced my two lung lobes. She crawled through all my organs and channels, both nervous system and circulatory system. I was totally fascinated and impressed. She gave me instructions: to remain still, attentive, and nonreactive. She gave me to understand that her colors were red and black and told me that my healing tool was a needle, which needed to have an eyelet. I was to use it on my skin until there was a drop of blood.

She showed me that everything having to do with nets and networks was her domain, including the internet, communications, and relational systems. Then I saw her masticating apparatus above me and it became clear that she wanted to devour me. I could not refuse her and I didn't want to. I was so impressed and fascinated by her that I wanted to give myself up to her completely, but I was afraid that "I" would get lost. I told her this and she responded by saying that I would be reborn with her power. It was both awesome and uncanny. Then she sucked me dry. I became bloodless and lifeless. Then I began to revive and I became Spider. I had the identity of a spider, even the body of a spider. I experienced some things from the point of view of Spider, for example the negative attitude most people have toward spiders and the grief around that. I saw the extreme loneliness resulting from such projections.

Then came the process of coniunctio that Ralph, the guide, had described. Hermes appeared from the right as a luminous orange-colored deity. I was anxious to know what Spider Grandmother would do now. I was afraid she might devour him. At that moment I recalled one of the alchemical illustrations of the coniunctio process, where the male body and female body merged together into one body with two heads. This is what happened. Spider was very still. I recalled that spider venom and quicksilver are two homeopathic remedies used in cases of sexual abuse, healing of male-female imbalance, and sexual healing in general.

I sensed the process was coming to an end, but I panicked because I seemed to be remaining in the identity of a spider. I felt I might be going insane and I asked for help. This was a crucial step because then the solution came immediately. The integrative process continued in lengthy and intense conversation with friends and allies over the following days. I was totally exhausted and emotionally stunned. More memories kept surfacing from lower depths of the psyche. It was very important to me that Ralph listened to my experience with total acceptance and supported my searching for and finding the meaning and significance of these very unexpected and yet profoundly healing experiences.

◆ ◆ ◆

Georgina ended her letter by relating that she spent months in discussions with friends and colleagues, integrating this powerful experience. She wrote that she felt she had acquired a powerful new spiritual and shamanic ally for both her personal growth and her work as a homeopathic physician and healer. It is important to recognize that the entire experience occurred during a group entheogenic ceremony in which the guidance was provided by me but there was no verbalization by or among participants. I was not aware of the nature of the visionary experience she was going through until she related it afterward. It was a true shamanic initiation.

6

Family Reconciliation through an Indigenous Ancestor

The practice of cultivating and maintaining one's connections with the spirit of deceased ancestors is probably the most significant feature that distinguishes the Western materially focused worldview from the indigenous-shamanic and Asian-culture worldviews. In these societies, which represent an absolute majority of the world's peoples, dying does not mean ceasing to exist; it only means a transformation of the soul's vehicle or vessel. I have sat in many Native American ceremonies and listened to the elders invoke the spirits of their deceased ancestors, asking for their blessings, in a natural, conversational, but respectful tone, as if these beings were in the room with them.

As we care for our children and grandchildren and want the best for them and to guide them along their life ways, so too do our ancestors, both the living and the dead, want to care for us and act as our back-up team in dealing with life's challenges. But, just like our family members who are still alive, our ancestors in the spirit world cannot or do not connect with us if we are not receptive to them. Communication with deceased ancestors would naturally be blocked if we are holding derogatory and judgmental attitudes toward them, and even more so if we believe they don't exist or that it's superstitious to have conversations with them. In group ceremonies and vision quests we have learned to invoke all of our ancestors, both the living and those on the other side, with simple, basic gratitude and respect for the gifts of life and guidance we have received from them.

When beginning to tune in to the soul connections with their grandparents (or even parents, at times), some people will object and say that they never knew them or that they were long deceased. But the vividness of the communication that can occur, whether with or without entheogenic amplification, confirms the reality of connections and communications that transcend the boundaries of death and birth. Although there are some exceptions, in my experience the ancestor spirits are usually delighted to be invited to connect—as most grandparents would be to connect with their grandchildren while still alive.

While I originally came to the practice of intentionally connecting with deceased ancestors through contact with Native American cultures, I felt supported and encouraged in this work through a connection with the work of Bert Hellinger. A German former priest and highly influential family-systems psychotherapist, Hellinger developed a method in which individuals can have a dialogue or encounter with relatives, whether alive or deceased. Family members speak through "representatives," who seem to embody these individuals in a mediumistic way through their relative placement in space and often without saying a word. The previously unconscious patterns of thought, feeling, and perception that come up can then often be very clearly seen, without any need for interpretive analysis. The individual concerned chooses representatives for his or her relatives from the audience, and these representatives are then positioned on the stage in such a way that physical space and placement mirrors and "shows" the psychic and emotional relationship patterns in the family.

When I learned about Hellinger's approach of setting up a circle of chosen representatives for an individual's relatives, both the living and the dead, on a public stage, I was confirmed in the approach I had developed of communing with the ancestors, whether personally acquainted or not, on a kind of inner stage. You face the souls or spirits of the ancestors, relatives, and elders directly, on a kind of inner mind-space or stage and dialogue with them telepathically, noting both questions and responses. We call this practice "connecting and reconciling with the ancestors."

Connecting and Reconciling with the Ancestors

After preparatory relaxing, deep easy breathing, and practicing the inner alchemical fires of purification, we invoke the souls of all members of the family. We invite them to a family council consisting of the basic triad of self, mother, and father; the two sets of grandparents and sometimes great-grandparents; and the aunts and uncles, especially if they were an active presence in the individual's childhood. Visual image perception of the individuals in the family soul council is not necessary. The inwardly formulated request or invitation results in an inner sense connection. We can sense the presence of someone near us without seeing them just as we could sense the presence of someone standing next to us in a totally dark room.

We ask the mother and her ancestors to stand on the person's left side and the father and his ancestors on the right side; the grandparents stand behind the parents. The person's own siblings and partners can stand next to the person. This was the inner family council practice we used in the following situation. If a therapist or guide who is not related to the family is participating in this ritual, it is important that he or she is also explicitly invited to this family council meeting and introduced to everyone along with explaining the purpose of the family gathering.

Trevor, who grew up in a Mormon family in Utah, was seeking to heal the damaged and difficult relationship he had with his mother, whom he remembered as being "hateful" to him while growing up. We tuned in to the ancestral council, where the three souls of mother, father, and child had agreed—and were still agreed—to incarnate together. Trevor wrote in his account after the amplified divination session:

I still really wasn't sold on reincarnation yet, but was allowing room for it. I saw my mother and father and I speaking in this together space. My mother had agreed to provide a spiritual structure for the family and my father had agreed to be my friend—my "buddy." This simple revelation brought on all sorts of emotion. This was why my mother was so insistent on me going to church and going on a mission, etc., when she had not been so with my brother and sister. Her not letting me go was perhaps the biggest problem I had with her. Now, I understood. It was part of her life mission, her operating system. She had promised to do it. She was simply fulfilling her promise. My father had also lived up to his word by being my buddy.

We then decided to further explore Trevor's connections with the two pairs of grandparents. We used a simple rattle as a support for the divination, as traditional shamans might use a drum or a rattle. Shaking a rattle and tuning in, with empathic communion, to his mother's parents, Trevor unexpectedly recalled that her father, his grandfather, used to take him out into nature, walking and fishing, when he was a boy. These experiences were long-forgotten pleasurable highlights of his childhood.

> *I immediately saw my mother's father, Otto, dressed in buckskin, dancing, singing, and crying in the dust with a rattle. The action and noise of the rattle was bringing in the spirits of my ancestors. The singing was a wailing that struck straight at my heart. Otto was doing work for me. Seeing Otto was a surprise because I had resented him for the lack of relationship he had with my mother. Additionally, I didn't have much respect for him intellectually, athletically, or financially. As I became active in the Mormon church I resented that he had not taken a role in the church. Now, there he was, dancing in the dust. I was overwhelmed by his spiritual power to call the spirits. I sensed his deep and powerful bond with the Earth.*

Trevor recalled how his grandfather Otto was always escaping to the mountains to fish. He remembered an experience he had with this grandfather when he was about ten or eleven. Trevor and his mother had traveled from San Francisco and were staying with Otto for a week or so. There was a creek running through his backyard that he had beautifully landscaped.

I played for a solid week in the creek. One afternoon, Otto took me on a hike into the canyon to find the source of the creek. We hiked on a narrow trail for a long time and found ourselves eventually sitting on a jagged ledge high in the wooded canyon, just admiring aspens and jagged rock formations. As I recalled Otto's deep love for the land I began to weep. I was so sorry I had discounted Otto. He was to be respected. I felt his love for the Earth was glorified, that his love for his family lived, and that he was actually doing spiritual work for our family. I was sobbing. It was intensely healing. I apologized to Grandpa Otto and vowed never to speak ill of him again.

Grandfather Otto, Trevor learned, was a Utah farm boy, who married socially upward into an urban family but was looked down upon by his wife's family for being a "country bumpkin," and possibly having "Indian" blood. This racist and classist superior attitude was passed on unconsciously to his daughter and his grandchild Trevor, who had held himself separate from his grandfather as he grew up and adopted the prejudiced attitudes of his generation.

Seeing his grandfather as a Native American—dancing, rattling, and chanting—reminded Trevor of the deep, loving connection with the natural world they had shared. As this connection to his partly indigenous ancestor came to the forefront of his consciousness, he saw the prejudicial attitudes of his mother's family as the source of her "hatefulness" and was able to connect with and honor his maternal lineage also more completely and more deeply.

7

Releasing the Daughter from Her Father's Youthful Tragic Obsession

Ursula, a physician in Germany, had participated in several of my alchemical divination circle groups but had still not been able to overcome her difficulty in establishing a lasting relationship with a man. She would repeatedly get involved with men who could not commit or who were weak and unstable. Although her father, Bernard, had been dead for ten years at the time we met, she told me she couldn't stop feeling a twinge of guilt every time she got seriously involved with a man. Although she knew it was irrational, she couldn't stop feeling that her involvement would somehow hurt her father. When, as a young woman in her twenties, she first got involved with a man, her father had become depressed and broke off all communication with her. Ten years after his death, Ursula still felt she was somehow possessed by her dead father's spirit and this was blocking her from establishing a relationship with a man. She wanted to release herself from that block. This was her intention for our healing work. I asked Ursula to relate her father's life story, as she had heard it from him.

As a young man, Bernard had served in the German army in the Russia campaign in the 1940s. At the end of the war he returned from imprisonment in the Siberian *gulag* prison system, where he had endured extreme physical and mental hardship. Bernard's story, as Ursula heard it from him when she was a young girl, was that just before he joined the army he had fallen in love with a young woman, and the memory of this love helped him survive the brutal hardships of the prison camp. However, Ursula and the rest of Bernard's family were never told what happened with this first love when Bernard returned from his imprisonment. He had some short-term unsatisfying relationships with women before eventually marrying the woman who became Ursula's mother. We decided to track further into Bernard's involvement with this young woman, which long preceded the birth of his daughter Ursula. One of the things I had learned from observing and studying Hellinger's family constellation work was that if there was a missing element in a story someone repeatedly told about their life, that missing element could well be the key to a healing resolution. In this case, the missing element was what actually happened between Bernard and his youthful love when he returned from the war.

We decided to invoke Ursula's ancestral soul council consisting of the souls of her mother, her father, and the respective grandparents to help her resolve the difficulties she was having in relationships with men. We used a mild amount of entheogenic medicine for amplification of awareness and prepared for the council meeting using the preliminary practice of relaxation and slowed breathing, followed by invoking the light of the Holy Spirit—using the Christian terminology in accord with her upbringing and family beliefs. I suggested that Ursula invite the souls to come to a meeting, much as she would invite her relatives to a gathering in her house.

The ancestral council readily assented to Ursula's request for help. I asked her to ask her ancestors if I, as her counselor, could participate in the meeting. I wanted to address questions to individuals in the council, especially her long-dead father Bernard, that Ursula would repeat in telepathic communion with the council of ancestors. She would then relate out loud the answers she received. I used the German formal address *Sie* to address her parents and grandparents. I was, after all, a visitor invited into the family circle. Ursula addressed her father Bernard as *Vati,* and used the familial *Du* in speaking with him. Ursula and I in this way pieced together the missing elements of Bernard's tragic story.

When we asked about Bernard's meeting with the young woman he fell in love with before he went off to the war, it turned out that he had never actually met or talked with her. He had only seen her from a distance, as she was in the same class as he at the university. He adored her and carried her image in his heart, and when he was in the gulag, the two things that helped him survive the rigors of the prison camp were his faith in God and his memory of this young woman. Ursula and I together asked him to describe conditions in the camp, which he did, hesitantly—the bitter cold, the hard labor, the hunger, the brutality of the guards. Many of the inmates died. In 1945, at the end of the war, the prisoners were released but not given transport back to Germany. Bernard, like many others, made his way on foot over a period of several weeks, surviving only through the occasional kindness of Russian peasants who gave him food and shelter. Both Ursula and I were stunned and deeply moved as her father's untold story came out to our sympathetic ears.

Bernard said, as transmitted through Ursula, that his amorous thoughts and dreams of the young woman with whom he had fallen in love helped him survive. They truly saved his life and his sanity. He had survived the gulag by remembering his secret love. Ursula and I both wanted to know more about the young woman and Bernard's relationship with her, as it saved his sanity and perhaps even his life. When we asked Bernard to say more we were told that he never actually dated the young woman, had never kissed her or declared his love. It was only her ideal image in his heart that gave him the strength to survive the brutal imprisonment.

We then inquired about what happened with his undeclared but life-saving love when he returned from the war. Hesitantly, in our mediated conversation, the answer came: the young woman in question was not interested in Bernard, and in fact she did not even remember him. They had never talked in any meaningful or intimate way. The love that had saved his life and his sanity was an idealized and imaginary affair. Bernard was devastated. He had forged this bond with her in his heart and mind, but she didn't want it or him. He became depressed, started drinking, had several affairs, and after a couple of years, met and married the woman who became Ursula's mother.

In the conversations with Bernard and the family council so far nobody had ever yet mentioned the young woman's name. Ursula and her family had never known the young woman's name or anything else about her, since Bernard had never mentioned it. When we asked in the family council of souls the answer came that her name was, in fact, "Ursula," the same name as Bernard's daughter. Somehow, Bernard had unconsciously transferred a life-saving possessive fixation from his early unfulfilled love to his daughter, born years later. She "belonged" to him, so to speak—she had after all saved his life.

Ursula then related to me the story her mother had told her of how she had gotten her name. Her mother and father had discussed several options for names during the pregnancy, and two days before the child was born, Bernard unexpectedly came to the mother and said, "The girl's name is Ursula." This was the moment at which the transfer of the obsessive fixation occurred—and it had never been released.

◆ ◆ ◆

To resolve this unfortunate obsession with a long-ago romantic infatuation and rejection I then suggested that Ursula address her father, mother, and the assembled family council of souls, speaking out loud as follows. She explained why she had called this family council, together with the therapist (me) who had been invited to participate, because she wanted to clear up a misconception that distorted healthy family connections. In front of the assembled ancestors and family members, Ursula expressed her gratitude to her father for finally communicating the painful story of his youthful secret love; her sympathy for his terrible suffering in the gulag; her acknowledgment of how the idealized, imaginary love connection with the other Ursula had saved his life and sanity; and her appreciation of how and why she, Ursula the daughter, had become a symbolic substitute for this idealized love that had evaporated into self-delusion. She then asked her father to release her from that long-dead connection, to affirm her freedom to choose a life mate for herself, and to give his blessing on her choice. To this heart-felt request, stated openly in front of the assembled ancestors, he readily assented and all the other ancestors expressed their support. The family meeting ended in a mood of quiet celebration.

A few days after this reconciliation ceremony was completed, Ursula told me she had phoned a new male friend to set up a rendezvous.

8

A Message of Peace Sent by a Dying Man to His Daughter

Andrea, a woman in her fifties with a chronic immune disorder, consulted me in order to identify and heal whatever familial karmic patterns were playing a role in the disease. We decided to do the process called Reconciliation with the Ancestors, in which we communicate intentionally at the soul level with both the living and the dead members of the family system.

Andrea's father and mother were a very young, newly married couple when she was born. Her father was an air-force flight instructor who accidentally crashed and died in his plane on a training mission when he was twenty-four, a few months after Andrea was born. Andrea's mother, who was nineteen at the time, was traumatized by the near-simultaneous birth of her child and accidental death of her husband. In her mind, she had been abandoned by her husband at her time of great need, with an infant to care for. She never recovered.

She became an alcoholic and neglectful of her children, bringing men friends home and leaving for days and weeks at a time. She sent her daughter to an orphanage school at the age of four. She never told Andrea anything about her father or what had happened to him. Granted, it would have been a difficult challenge to explain to a young child, but as Andrea grew older, her mother was too far gone into alcoholic disconnect to ever try to heal this family tragedy. Since no one ever told her the true story about her parents, Andrea absorbed the message that her father had abandoned the family and followed her mother's pattern of reckless immaturity. At age fourteen, she ran away from home with her boyfriend, and in her early twenties, she became pregnant with a son.

When she consulted me, she was in her fifties, had a fulfilling career as an interior designer, and was happily married. In general, it has been my practice to recommend delving into parental or ancestral karmic entanglements only when the individual concerned is in a stable and supportive family situation. It seems natural that as we move into the second half of our life we become more motivated to try to heal long-standing differences or residual difficulties with parents and grandparents. That's why Andrea decided to do the ancestral reconciliation ritual both with her mother and her father, whom she had never known in person. A small amount of amplification with an empathogenic substance was used to deepen the soul connection with the ancestors.

~᷉

Ritual of Healing and Reconciliation
with the Ancestors

By way of preparation, we focus and center ourselves with sensing awareness and purifying light-fire energy in the heart center, the pelvic-abdominal center, the head center, and the "upper room" center above the top of the head. A sphere of inner light-fire about three feet in diameter is ignited in each of these four centers, radiating the alchemical fire of purification in all directions—right and left, forward and backward, upward and downward. We declare the intention that we are inviting family members and ancestors to a ritual of reconciliation for the sake of the individual who is calling this council. Whatever divine spirit or deity figure the individual feels most connected with is asked to bless the healing ceremony with their presence and guidance. Any animal spirits that the core person has a relationship with through previous shamanic work can also be invited to be present.

The assembly of ancestral souls is arranged in concentric semicircles facing the core individual in the center—the mother and her ancestors on the left, the father and his ancestors to the right. Siblings of the mother and father, i.e., aunts and uncles of the core individual, are invited to stand next to mother and father. The two sets of grandparents are invited to stand behind the parents. Siblings who grew up together with the core individual are invited to stand next to him or her. The husband, wife, or partner of the core individual stand next to him or her, facing the assembly of ancestors. It is up to the person in the situation whether former spouses are invited into the council, but it is essential that any partners, past or present, who are coparents of children with the core person be invited. The children can assume a place in front of the individual who is the convener of this council.

It is crucially important that everyone who is related by birth to the central trio of mother, father, and child be invited to participate in the family council—even if, as people sometimes say, they "never knew" them or they died before the person's birth. As the work of Bert Hellinger and other family-systems therapists has demonstrated, no one who is related should be excluded—even if, or perhaps especially if, that individual performed immoral or hateful actions, which led to them being "never spoken of" in the family. In fact, it is precisely such exclusions from the family system, based on overwhelming grief or unresolved conflicts, that often turn out to be an important causal factor in interpersonal or intrapsychic difficulties.

We are talking here about the level of soul connection—a level at which negativity, dislike, bad personality traits, and so on are irrelevant. We are not approving or disapproving anyone's personal actions or attitudes. We are recognizing and acknowledging the familial connection based on the incarnating choices made by immortal souls and inviting all related souls to participate in a healing ritual. The extent to which they do so is of course up to them, and we may not know, at the level of personality, the degree of that participation. But as Hellinger's work has shown, and as exemplified in the previous story, there can sometimes be crucially important family secrets unknown to the person involved, which can come to light in this way.

Once the two sides of the family and their ancestors are assembled in this way, the core individual makes the following statements of acknowledgment and gratitude, separately to each of the two sets of ancestors. Unlike divinations, which are questions designed to elicit insight or understanding, these statements are affirmations of core connections. People feel empowered when they are making them, authentically and from the heart, whether silently or aloud, because they affirm the soul connection. The soul connection is deeper and more secure than all the confused and illusory overlays of personality and conditioning. I will give below the statements as they would be addressed to one of the parents and then repeated, with the appropriate changes in wording, for the other.

In addressing the mother and father in this family council of souls, we call the parents "Mother" and "Father" rather than terms such as "Mom" or "Dad" because the latter are the words used by a child, and we are talking here about an interaction between adults. The soul of a child is an equal in stature, wisdom, and worth to the parental soul. I also recommend that one use the mother's or father's first name, e.g., William or Janet. This acknowledges that the individual concerned had and has an identity, a history, and a sense of who they are, beyond being the mother or father. People have often reported, in my groups, how important it was in their relationship with a parent to acknowledge and appreciate that the parent had a life before and beyond parenthood. So we bow with respect and say:

- "[Name], Mother, Grandmother, Grandfather—I honor you and thank you for the thread of life that you have passed on to me." [For those who have children, add: "And that I, in turn, am passing on to my children and descendants."]
- "Whatever I have received from you and through you, both the strengths and the weaknesses, I accept unconditionally and at the full price that it cost you. I am weaving these patterns into the ongoing tapestry of my life."

- "You will always have a place in my heart. There will always be a place for you at our family table."
- "I am grateful to you for the positive qualities and strengths that I have received from you, by inheritance or by example." [Here people can specify and list the good qualities they are glad to have received.] "If I find anything that I have taken on from you that does not further my soul's purpose or learning, I will not continue to carry it forward."

This last statement is the crucial resolution to a difficulty that plagues so many relationships between grown-up children and their parents. We don't need to reject the parents in order to reject certain traits in them that we find objectionable. We don't even need to reject or fight against the objectionable traits—we can just let them be and not take them on, or no longer carry them forward. Character traits are like the clothes we were obliged or induced to wear when we were children. We adopted these traits, unconsciously and unintentionally, in our childhood years because there was no alternative choice, and we needed the parents' protection and guidance. But we can let them go, like our childhood clothes, if we find we don't need or want them anymore. This absolutely does not mean rejecting the parent or not loving them. On the contrary, it can only be really done with love, for as we know, hatred is as strong a binding glue as love. So we can say—alternatively or in addition:

- "I will always cherish you and be grateful for your protection and guidance in my early life. This particular quality or trait that I inadvertently took on from you [name the trait] I am now just leaving it here."

At the end of the reconciliation ritual, we ask the ancestors to reposition themselves. The mother and her ancestors are asked to stand behind on the left. The father and his ancestors are asked to stand behind on the right-hand side. We can ask the parents and other ancestors to provide ongoing guidance, counsel, and support in life, as we request. When doing this ritual practice, especially when connecting with deceased ancestors that they hadn't thought much about at all, people often reported a surprisingly warm and supportive response from long ignored or forgotten ancestors that were pleased to be recognized and asked to lend their moral support.

In our session, Andrea first performed the reconciliation divination with her mother and the maternal ancestors. At the time, Andrea was taking care of her aged, invalid mother, who lived near her and her husband. In the healing ritual she invoked the souls in the maternal lineage and expressed recognition of the familial connection and acceptance of what happened—without judgment or blame. As we went through the steps of this reconciliation ritual Andrea, inwardly connected with her mother, experienced moving from a place of bitterness and anger to a place of peace and compassion.

I then guided Andrea into the parallel reconciliation process with her father. Addressing him at the level of soul and speaking from the heart, she expressed gratitude for receiving the thread of life from him and his ancestors. She said: "I give you now a place in my heart. Sooner or later I too will die, as you did." She told him she was no longer blaming him, realizing that when she was a child she had adopted the belief that he had abandoned the family in the absence of any communication from her mother about his life or his fate.

Andrea's story was one of several I have heard that convinced me of the importance of a parent communicating honestly with a child when a parent, grandparent, or sibling dies, in whatever language is appropriate for the child. To say nothing about it can provoke guilt in the child, who may believe that they were somehow responsible for the death or disappearance of a family member. Needless to say, it is difficult for a parent to talk with a child about the death of a family member. Andrea's mother had never mentioned her father or told her anything about him because she was too caught up in her own grief and self-pity. The consequence of not doing so, however, can be lifelong depression, guilt, or self-destructive behavior.

In the course of our work together on connecting with her father Andrea related the following recurrent, mysterious dream she had when she was an adolescent.

I am in an airplane, sitting next to the pilot in the cockpit. Suddenly, the engines die and the plane begins to fall to earth. The pilot makes several attempts to restart the engines, but they fail. The plane starts to fall. It is a long, long fall. We keep falling. Finally, I clearly see the ground below. My impulse is to close my eyes to prepare for the impact, but what I see is so beautiful I want to leave them open and look at the landscape. I see where earth and sky meet. I feel very calm and unafraid. I relax and wait. Miraculously, there is no impact. The landscape before me is suffused with white light, growing brighter, increasingly glowing. As I enter, I feel a profound sense of peace, which stays with me as I wake up.

Andrea realized then that her father had been sending her, when she was a young person, these messages concerning his absence. He wanted to reassure her that he did not mean to "abandon" her and her mother. He wanted to help her understand that his dying went beyond the place of terror to a place of peace. She was able then to express her long-delayed gratitude to his soul for this gift. He came to live with her in Spirit, even as her aging, invalid mother returned to live with her in body.

◆ ◆ ◆

The stories in the previous three chapters have shown how unconscious patterns from the lives of parents and grandparents can affect present-life circumstances and challenges, both negatively and positively. In the life stories related in the following four chapters we see how circumstances from previous incarnations can function as unconscious karmic undercurrents of thought, feeling, and behavior in the present, and can best be healed by intentional recognition.

9

The Lost Beloved Brother Returned as the Son

Tobias, a physician in Germany, consulted me for psychedelic psychotherapy with the intention of gaining insight into and healing of two issues. One was his troubled relationship with his boss at the hospital where he worked; the other was feeling that his marriage was stuck because of their inability to have children. Tobias was an only child, and his childhood had been lonely, as both parents were preoccupied with their own affairs and emotionally distant. In the course of our initial conversation, Tobias told me that his father used to say to him, jokingly, "I'm not actually your father, ha, ha." This remark, which was apparently repeated more than once, greatly disturbed the young boy, since he feared that his already distant father might abandon him completely. As I had learned from the work of Bert Hellinger, the insensitive joke could be a clue that something was "off" in the ancestral family constellation.

When I inquired into Tobias's family history on the paternal side, Tobias related that his father had been traumatized by losing his beloved older brother when he was five, and his father (Tobias's grandfather) when he was fifteen—thus losing both his adult male role models during childhood. I guided Tobias to invoke the council of ancestral souls, which includes, at minimum, the souls of the two parents and the two sets of grandparents. Subsequently, we also invoked the council of guiding spirits.

The Council of Ancestors and the Council of Spirit Guides

My statements in this area are based on more than thirty years of experience and observation in past-life therapy and are consistent with, though not derived from, the writings of a number of psychics and regression therapists including Winafred Lucas, Denys Kelsey, Joan Grant, Kurt Leland, Michael Newton, Sylvia Browne, Caroline Myss, and others. There are two groups of supportive and guiding souls and spirits that accompany us throughout our lives: the council of ancestors and the council of spirit guides. Both offer counsel when requested, although they do not compel us or interfere in any way with our free-will choices. We may be only intermittently aware of them consciously, or even not at all, as they guide and counsel us through dreams and intuitions. Once we accept the reality of their presence, we can, through practice, increase our recall and conscious reception of their guidance and counsel.

The *council of ancestors* consists of the souls—not the personalities—of parents and grandparents on the mother's and the father's side, sometimes including ancestors further back in the genetic lineage. The ancestral family council may also include the siblings of the parents. This is the council of the souls that accompany us throughout the present lifetime and can guide us and consult with us on issues and questions of our current incarnation. It does not matter if the parents and grandparents are personally conscious of their role at the level of soul—although of course parents are notoriously and sometimes excessively concerned with guiding their offspring. Maybe this is the reason why we tend to have a clearer and less cluttered connection with parental and ancestral souls after they are dead and no longer so preoccupied with guiding us in the details of our pathways in life.

The depth of our personal connection with different ancestors may vary greatly—we naturally feel closer to some than to others. It is also important to remember that our ancestors are (or were) not necessarily wise or spiritual persons in life. But because they are on the other side of the divide of life and death, they may be able to convey helpful perspectives and even family secrets unknown to the surviving family members. To give just one example: if there are doubts in a person's mind as to who their father really is, only a conscious interaction with the mother's soul can reveal the truth, either before or after death. Thus, the ancestral souls can be particularly helpful in unraveling the sometimes confused and hidden lines of family karma.

The *council of spirit guides,* which is usually perceived as somehow "higher" and more remote than the ancestral council, consists of a group of guides or spiritual teachers, some human, some perhaps shamanic power animals or deity spirits known to us through myth and visionary experience. These are the soul-spirits that know us and accompany us through many lives in different times and places. They meet with us in the afterlife when the time comes for the life review and an assessment of what we learned in the earth life just ended and what projects and tasks we have in the higher worlds. This is the council of beings that can give us the knowledge of past incarnations that may be playing a role in the present situation and prepare us for possible future incarnations. Our perception of this higher council of guides tends to be less vivid and detailed than our awareness of the ancestral council. But here too, with practice, the connections and guidance received can become clearer and more definite. In my experience there is usually no overlap between the two councils—although there are possible exceptions, such as could occur if one of the ancestors is also an important spirit guide.

◆ ◆ ◆

After we had done the preparatory meditation with the light-fire energy radiating out from the heart center and had established the empathic soul communion with his father's spirit in the context of the council of ancestors, Tobias and I held the question in our minds about the significance of Tobias's father's hurtful remark to his son. Following an unexpected intuitive prompting, I asked if perhaps Tobias was the reincarnation of his father's beloved older brother, who had died when the father was teenager. Tobias's eyes brimmed with tears of emotion at this question, seeming to confirm the soul connection. This would explain the strange "joke": his father, although having no belief system or understanding concerning reincarnation, nevertheless somehow "knew" the soul connection between his long-dead brother and his son and tried to convey it to his son, albeit in a clumsy, awkward way. After this revelation, Tobias felt reconciled with his father in a much deeper way.

I do not know if this is generally true, but it occurred to me after hearing this story that perhaps when a child dies it is more likely to seek a subsequent reincarnation in the same family—as if to repair a ruptured relationship with the same parents and siblings. Many of the reincarnation stories collected by Ian Stevenson from children in India seem to confirm this notion. These children remembered dying while being a child and coming back to that same family—as if to fulfill some basic agreement to be together in that family.

◆ ◆ ◆

Seeking a deeper understanding of the roots of Tobias's present difficulties with his boss, we then decided to consult the combined council of ancestors and council of spiritual guides. We decided to inquire if there was a past-life connection between the two of them. Tobias's other question about the difficulty he and his wife were experiencing in conceiving children was also on the agenda.

We used the following method of finding access to a past-life memory. It usually works best if the guide verbalizes the questions and the seeker verbalizes the answers out loud, which helps to consolidate the perception. The images seem to emerge out of a kind of liquid solution, somewhat like a photographic print that gradually emerges and consolidates from a liquid suspension. Sometimes a person will say that they're not getting anything, but then after further relaxation and deep breathing, a stream of images emerges. It's also helpful not to tighten the physical eyes as if trying to focus—instead, let the eyes relax and go out of focus. You don't need or use the physical eyes for inner seeing anyway—as many stories of blind prophets and seers attest.

～

Accessing a
Past-Life Memory

Center your awareness with deepening breath in the heart-center field and expand the purifying light-fire energy stream spherically in all directions: backward and forward, upward and downward, left and right. Visualize yourself in a large, lighted dome-shaped cave, filled with a warm, purifying, and illuminating fire in the center. Your Higher Self envelops you with a protective aura field of golden light. Around you in concentric circles are all your familial ancestors and both human and nonhuman relations, channeling their support. Toward the back of the cave, corresponding anatomically to the inside back wall of the chest cavity, there are three doorways. The one on the left back side leads to the mother's ancestors, the one on the right back side to the father's family.

We now concentrate on the cave tunnel entrance directly behind the center of the chest, which will lead you to a past life that is connected in some way to the divination question that you are asking. A soft drum beat or rattle may accompany you as you walk confidently into the dark entrance of the cave and proceed for a few minutes until you emerge out into an open landscape. Begin by looking down at your feet—are you barefoot or are you wearing shoes? As you move your gaze up your legs—are you a woman or a man? What are you wearing? What color is your clothing? What is the size and stature of your body? Are you carrying or holding anything? Do you have something on your head? After scanning your whole body, look around at the landscape. Where are you? What kind of environment are you in? What is going on? Are there others around you?

Once one is connected to this question-and-answer process, it can go fairly quickly. It is not necessary to ask all the questions listed above—some people find themselves in an obviously different lifetime and place as soon as they emerge from the dark cave or tunnel. For others, it is helpful to get more detailed descriptions of the clothing, the landscape, the presence of others, and so forth until there is a kind of crystallization of the process. It's as if the person is looking through a kind of optical device through which they can see the scenes from their other life as vividly as memories from their present life.

Upon emerging out of the cave tunnel, Tobias found himself standing, sword in hand, on a medieval battlefield where a battle had just taken place. It was a desolate scene of carnage and destruction, and he was one of the last men left standing. Emotionally, he was devastated. Tobias knew that in that life he was a vassal knight, fighting battles on behalf of his liege lord. I asked Tobias whether this liege lord, on whose behalf he was fighting, was also incarnated in his present life. He answered immediately that it was his present boss with whom he had the difficult relationship.

We then inquired farther back in that life of fighting to the time before this last battle and found a prior campaign, or perhaps it was earlier in the same campaign, in which he was fighting for this same liege lord. The knight's own home castle had been destroyed and his wife and children killed while he was off fighting. His wife in that life was his wife again in his present life, the one with whom he could not have children.

We both saw clearly how Tobias's grief over the loss of his family was compounded by his guilt over having failed to protect them. There was deep despair that his loyal knightly service to his liege lord had led to the loss of everyone he held dear in his life. He saw how both the loss of his family and his conflicted loyalty to his superior had carried over to his present life—probably to further process the karmic residues and lessons learned.

In past-life regressions I customarily go back to the individual's early life and family of origin to get a more complete sense of the life story. We did not do that in this instance. We also did not review the manner of his death or how old he was when it occurred, although these details can also be very revealing. Because of the dominance of tragic issues of guilt, loss, and the death of loved ones, I felt it was important to complete the divination by going to the combined council of ancestral souls and guiding spirits. I always emphasize that the individual is an equal member of both these councils, whose task it is not to judge or condemn but to evaluate the lessons learned and karmic debts incurred. In the hundreds of divinations to such post-death council meetings, I and my fellow explorers have never found any hint of condemnation or punishment from the ancestors and spirit guides.

The ancestral and guiding spirit councils review the life together with an attitude of profound compassion and objectivity, asking what the soul's purposes and visions in that life had been, what was learned, and what remains to be learned in possible future lives—always making it clear that it is we ourselves who are also making these evaluations and choices. Tobias met with the ancestral and guiding spirit councils and reviewed again the karmic consequences of the way of life and death in that life of knighthood, loyalty, and battle. Meeting in council with the souls of the others—his wife and family and his boss—enabled him to release himself from the self-punitive guilt over his excessive loyalty and the loss of his loved ones.

10

Releasing Guilt in the Healing Temple of Justice

Peter, a Swiss man in his sixties, and his wife participated in a number of the circle workshops I conducted in Germany, Switzerland, and Sweden that focused on the healing methods we call *alchemical divination,* usually done with entheogenic amplification. In the group circle workshops we go through guided healing divinations in which memory images from childhood, from the prenatal period, and from previous lives may come up. But since participants are in a group ceremony in which there is no talking, such images cannot be pursued in detail, as is possible in individual reincarnation therapy. Peter had told me, and written in a letter, that he was disturbed by repeated past-life flashbacks in his dreams and meditations and in our group ceremonies. He experienced momentary flashbacks to a past life in which he had experienced the savagery and inhumanity of war, which clearly still disturbed him. The repetitiveness of these traumatic visions and memories suggested an unresolved issue left over from that life. We decided to do an individual past-life regression divination, so I could guide him to focus on the back and forth of questions posed and answers received.

Just as traumatic events in childhood or in the prenatal period may persist in adult memories as confused, anxious, or even terrifying fragments of thoughts, images, feelings, and sensations in dreams and nightmares mixed with guilt and shame and terror, we may also find them linking back to another life. In my practice, if the causal factors of a present symptom or dysfunctional thought-image complex are not found in a search through childhood, birth trauma, prenatal conditions, conception, and familial ancestral patterns we resort to inquiring into past-life connections. For this to be effective as a therapeutic practice, one does not need to believe in reincarnation or have a theoretical system that explains how it works. One just needs to be open to the possibility.

The taboo on accepting reincarnation and past-life karma in Western culture is very strong, dating back 1,500 years to the First Council of Nicaea, which dictated that after we die, there are only three options for us—heaven, hell, or purgatory. These options are not really a matter of choice but are strictly determined by an accounting of our sins and virtues. The taboo against reincarnation was seeded into the culture as a power maneuver by the church, which wanted people to focus on dealing with, and paying for, their sins in this life. The denial of reincarnation still lingers with surprisingly unexamined tenacity in modern minds—even in those no longer identified with Christianity or any other religion.

That we live many lifetimes working out the karmic consequences of our actions is accepted as a matter of fact, not belief, in the majority of the world's cultures and societies and always has been.

It is also referred to openly in both the Old and New Testaments of the Bible. In order to work with past-life memories in psychotherapy, one need only stop dismissing or denying reincarnation and be open to the possibility. Recognizing that the principle of karma extends beyond death across multiple lifetimes and afterlife conditions would put a powerful brake on the heedless and arrogant indulgence in destruction and violence that plagues the modern world, despite all its astonishing technical creativity and genius.

Peter had already determined, in his previous explorations, that he had a past life in which he was the mayor of a small village on the Austrian-Czechoslovakian border, in the Siebengebirge ("Seven Mountains") range. It was a period during the 1920s and '30s. The mayor, whose name was Andrej, was married and had five children, and he was respected as someone who could mediate conflicts. Peter said, "My wife in my present life also lived in this village. She was a healer, and we had an inner connection."

When the Germans invaded Czechoslovakia in 1939, a group of partisans, including two of Andrej's sons, formed a resistance movement. The Germans wanted the mayor to give them the names of the fighters in the resistance and promised that, if he named names, the village would not be harmed.

> "I gave them the names, and then they went ahead and executed everyone anyway. I was betrayed. I saw the first execution in the village center and felt a tight ball of rage, frustration, and guilt as I died. I know they executed all the men in the village." His last thought in that life before he himself was executed was, "something like this should never happen—the betrayal and destruction of a whole village, for which I had responsibility."

One of the key factors that determines whether a past-life trauma will carry over into the present life is if the death in the past life was violent and unexpected rather than peaceful and prepared. This is the basic reason why world religions and spiritual traditions emphasize preparation for a peaceful, spiritually oriented death in their various versions of Books of the Dead. This is also why, when working with past-life psychotherapy, I have always tried to include a regression to determine the timing and manner of the death in the past life.

With my guidance and participant observation, Peter had practiced regression meditations with the attitude of an empathic observer several times. As previously described, the practice of the empathic observer or compassionate witness involves looking at the whole situation—both internal-subjective and external-objective—with the neutrality of the witness/observer: neither for nor against nor pulling away from the situation but staying with it and allowing oneself to perceive and recognize all aspects of it, while remaining grounded, balanced, and connected to Spirit or Higher Self. But the attitude of the balanced observer/witness by itself has a tendency to become detached, aloof, indifferent, and cold. So, as the Buddhists say, wisdom and compassion are to be practiced together, the observer attitude together with empathy. Empathy stays centered in the heart space and grounded. With this attitude Peter was able to look at the whole terrible past-life scene with a compassionate attitude for his past and present selves. "I could recognize and remember it, but with empathy, and without identifying."

Peter was then guided in a meditative trance state to the council of ancestral souls. As he wrote in his description of the process afterward,

I knew I was in the interlife period between that life and my present life. There were these schematic figures, moving back and forth gently like plants under water. There was a great sphere radiating blue light, the wisdom light of truth. Everything was very calm and peaceful. The karmic knots, the complex of thoughts and feelings that had carried over from the past betrayal, were being dissolved and transformed by the blue light-fire in my heart center.

But there was some resistance. Peter asked himself why he had been holding on to this story for so long. I told him that we have found that a strong negative emotion, whether fear or rage, at the moment of death may be carried over into the next life. The answer came that it was his rage at the betrayal of his word of honor, which had such terrible, tragic consequences.

With this recognition, as we continued tuning in with the council of ancestral souls, he found no rage or thought of revenge, only a need and wish for closure and balancing. We both realized he had started to tune in to the higher council of spirit guides, who see the karmic patterns over many lifetimes and involving whole groups of people, as would be expected in a war situation. Peter felt a mood of peacefulness come through from the two councils combined, the ancestors and the spiritual guides, infusing into his present awareness and personality, his mind, emotions, and perceptions. He wrote:

The soul council had several layers. First, there were my familial ancestors and then a kind of mythic white-haired Wise Old Man and also the Lady Fatima of the Springs, with her green stone. In the council of guiding souls I also recognized Nicholas von Flue, a spiritual teacher from the Middle Ages in Switzerland, whom I had long admired.

As Peter continued his account, he described a large gathering of human souls, alive beyond earthly life, as well as the guides and teachers with whom he was connected.

All 120 souls of those who were my responsibility and who were killed in that action were invited to the gathering and came. They had lost their lives, for which I felt responsible. I was guided to beam light and empathy at them. It was a warm and healing spiritual fire. No one blamed me or made any kind of accusation at me for what I did. I realized it was presumptuous of me to blame myself.

This last statement is very significant because our conditioned guilt mechanisms tend to ascribe much more personal responsibility than is really warranted. It was, after all, a war situation in which Peter and his compatriots were killed by an overwhelming enemy force.

At my urging and with the support of the greater council of spirit guides, Peter then also invited the souls of the German soldiers who had carried out the massacre to meet with and join a larger combined gathering of souls. Tuning in to the soldiers' state of consciousness at the time of the massacre, he realized that they were just soldiers, obediently and mindlessly carrying out the work they were commanded to do. They had no personal hatred toward him and no concern for their victims either. He began to sense and describe a larger web of fate, a force of destiny that included both victims and perpetrators. Peter kept reminding himself of his chosen mantra of *freudige Gelassenheit* (joyful serenity) to stay centered in the consciousness of soul and Higher Self.

The guide told me about the South African Truth and Reconciliation Commissions, where perpetrators and victims of the years of oppression and murder sat together in council, and how healing it was for the former victims to be heard by the former perpetrators, who had previously demeaned them and denied their humanity. The blue sphere of wisdom light, associated with the goddess Sophia, hovered above the council. The guide invited me to speak for the victims who were killed: "It was terrible, to be ripped out of this world so violently, away from the Earth and our fellow human beings." And to speak also for the soldiers who carried out the killing: "It was our work task, we had to do it, and we did no more and no less."

Peter noted that in this ancestral and guiding council meeting both victims and killers were peaceful but without human emotions. The individuals in both groups said that at the time of the massacre, they had already been experiencing war for some time and that something in them died in the war. They all had scars and wounds from that. In his later account, Peter wrote:

Hearing that, I felt close to the killers. We all participated in a common fate, beyond victims and perpetrators. There was a feeling like a kind of dance of life, of ending war and of peace. Very softly and quietly, angels of peace and of justice were also attending, beaming out soothing, calming vibration waves. These energies were emanating from above and pouring into the souls now still (or again) living in human bodies, including mine. I rested for a long time in this healing temple of justice and peace.

11

A Mother's Past-Life Deathbed Vow Carried Over

Serena, who came from a wealthy family on her mother's side, consulted me because she felt guilty and despondent over her needy and invalid father, whom I'll call William. Growing up she felt very close to her father. When she was around eight or nine years old, her parents had struggled through a painful divorce. She told me she remembered a vow she inwardly made to her father at that time: "I'll always take care of you." It was a strange statement for a young girl to make in relation to her father, and it alerted me to the possibility of a "bleed through" from another life. In a material sense, Serena's family was providing for William, and yet her childhood guilt feelings about him persisted, along with obsessive thoughts that he needed her.

I had learned from previous work that seemingly unexplained inversions of the usual parent-child relationship could point to an unconscious replay of an unresolved dilemma from a past life. I suggested to Serena that here was a question that called for a past-life divination, since there was nothing in the present-life situation that indicated her father needed caretaking from his own daughter or that she was responsible for him—especially when she was still a child. We decided to do a past-life divination, and I suggested that Serena ask her wise Higher Self the following question: "Where did my impulse and vow as a young child to take care of my adult father come from?"

Drinking from Mimir's Well
of Remembrance

In the course of writing my book on Norse-Germanic mythology, *The Well of Remembrance,* I had come to realize that many of the poetic stories told in the myths contained coded metaphoric references to divination practices that could still be used in modern times. The Nordic seers and poetic storytellers used the metaphoric image of a well, situated at the foot of the world tree, to refer to divination practices. The world tree is a symbolic image of the world axis—in modern terms this is the axis of the spinning Earth globe, giving us one of our basic measures of time, the ceaseless cycle of night and day. The world tree also symbolizes the central vertical axis of the body—we center ourselves on this axis when we practice divination while seated in a centered, meditative posture. *Mimir,* whose name means "memory" in the old Norse language, was the ancient wise giant who dwelled at the roots of the world tree and guarded the well of remembrance. It was said that if you wanted to remember and reconnect with your past or the past of your family and your world by drinking from Mimir's well, you had to ask Mimir for permission and pay the price he demanded.

In the old myths we are told that the truth-seeking god Odin paid the price of one eye, and so he became the one-eyed god who roamed the Earth and the hidden worlds, seeking knowledge of the past and the future. While an eye may seem a steep price to pay for access to hidden knowledge of the past, it does convey the value the ancient seers and seekers put on real and true knowledge of the past, both personal and planetary. In the divinations using this mythic image to access knowledge of the past we always invoke the guidance and permission of Mimir the Rememberer: we declare our intention or state our question, and we humbly and sincerely ask what we need to pay.

Our language can often reveal the hidden meaning in ancient metaphors. The answer we always received to our question to Mimir about payment was that we just need to *pay attention*. In other words, the divination is not a passive matter, like looking through a photo album. We invoke our own Higher Self, get clear about what questions we are asking, and pay attention to what we see or hear or find. Interestingly, in German one says *die Aufmerksamkeit schenken,* literally, "giving the gift of attention." Whether as gift or as payment, attending is an intentional double process of first asking and then receiving the answers or the guidance.

Having received permission from Mimir, we would find ourselves at the well, or sometimes it was said to be a spring, at the foot of the world tree. Our own vertical spinal axis is aligned with the cosmic world axis. The roots of the tree are aligned with what is called in yoga the *root chakra* at the base of the spine; the crown of the tree is aligned with what is called the *crown chakra* at the top of the head. The personal and the planetary, "the above and the below," are synchronized and aligned. The divination process consists of lowering an imaginary cup into the well of memories—or one can just use cupped hands to scoop up some of the water—raising it up to the mouth and drinking it down, so the memories are assimilated into present body-mind awareness. One can lower and raise the cup to drink repeatedly in the course of connecting with a series of memory images. The depth of the well of remembrance is the measure of time. To access prenatal memories we have to go deeper down than for childhood memories. For access to past-life memories we go deeper still.

◆ ◆ ◆

In the divination with Serena, we first invoked the souls of all her ancestors and family, her animal and plant allies, and her chosen deity spirits. She entered into a light meditative trance, amplified by a small amount of psilocybe mushrooms. I guided Serena to situate herself at the foot of the great world tree, coinciding with her own spinal axis tree, to invoke the spirit of Mimir the Rememberer and to ask the question concerning her need to care for her father. As she lowered a cup into the well of memories, deeper than her current life:

> She found herself in a life as a peasant maid on a farm, in Northern Europe somewhere, maybe Sweden, living on her own. She has a young son, who she knows immediately is her father, William, in her present life. She is desperately poor with no resources. Her son's father is gone. Perhaps he was the landowner or someone from his family who took advantage of the maid. She and her son are living in a small hut or hovel on the land, somehow scraping by. The girl vowed to herself to take care of the boy, no matter what. As the boy grows up he turns out to be retarded or handicapped in some way, not capable of taking care of himself. Although desperately poor,

she continues to take care of her son, affirming the vow, "I'll always take care of you."

So this was the answer to her question about the origin of this obligation she felt to take care of William—then her son, now her father. Vows are deeper than promises, and a mother's vow to her child is perhaps the deepest of all, whether spoken out loud or not. A vow invokes the soul connection between them and thus can transcend the current lifetime, if it is not intentionally revoked or resolved. In that past life, it was not revoked or released by the natural circumstances of life because at the end of that past life the impoverished mother felt her son still needed her care.

As usual in such divinations, I guided Serena to review the end of that past life.

Going forward to the end of that other life, the woman is on her deathbed, in her fifties, and the son, now an adult, still lives with her, as he is still not quite capable of taking care of himself. So on her deathbed she affirms her vow that "I'll always take care of you."

This was the deathbed vow that was carried over. A mother who dies in the presence of a normal adult child would not make such a vow—it would be unnecessary and inappropriate. But if the child, now adult, still needs care, the mother's concern and promise makes sense in the context of that life. But deathbed vows are serious matters and would likely be carried over into a subsequent life or lives, if not repealed or released in some way.

To release Serena from the residual guilt over not being able to keep an impossible promise to her son, we created a *ceremony of reconciliation.* All of Serena's and William's family members—parents, grandparents and siblings, those still alive and those already in the spirit world—were invited and took their place in a great circular council of souls. I suggested to Serena that she address the soul who was her father, William, in the present life and was her son in the past life, speaking authentically and from the heart: "You will always have a place in my heart."

The power of this statement, affirming the loving familial connection between souls, is that it doesn't have any limiting or specifying conditions. Not necessarily the biggest or the closest or most important place—but a place nonetheless. Serena repeated the phrase, addressing William in their present-life situation of an adult woman speaking to her aging father, who had fallen on hard times financially and was in poor health.

Then there was a beautiful moment when Serena spontaneously added the phrase, "And you will always have a place at our table," addressing her present-life father, with the echo of her past-life son. This additional statement affirmed the belongingness of the family to share a meal together, while respecting the dignity of the other as an adult to take care of himself. The financial support of her father William was worked out by agreements made in an actual family council. Serena was freed from her strange compulsion to personally continue to emotionally nurture her father in this life.

12

The Liberating Death of a Persecuted Witch Healer

Bella, a German physician and gynecologist, had a recurring intrusive image, in nightmarish dreams and altered states of high stress, of being persecuted as a witch. She knew it was a flash-back to a past life somewhere in Europe in the early Middle Ages—the time of the Inquisition and the murder of millions of witches, the "wise women" healers and midwives. In her mind's eye she would see a murderous throng of villagers, men and women, some armed with pitchforks and sticks, running after her crying, *"Hexe, Hexe."* Some of the men, she knew and felt, projected lustful and violent fantasies at her. As she ran from the throng, her heart was filled with terror and hatred. Then the visions would stop or she would wake from the nightmare. There never seemed to be any resolution or comple-tion. The same scenario would play itself out in her fantasy mind or dream, sometimes during group experiences with entheogens, again and again. She asked for help in releasing this recurrent nightmare from her memory and mind.

As discussed in previous chapters, intrusive flashbacks from a past incarnation seem to appear most often in those people whose death in the past life was unexpected and filled with negative emotions because of war or criminality. Because in group circle divinations each person focuses inwardly on their own experience and well-defended traumatic memories tend to stay out of direct awareness, we concluded that a focused individual memory divination to this past life was indicated.

In the alchemical and shamanic groups I've conducted both in Europe and the United States over the past thirty years, past-life memories of experiences in the torture chambers of the Inquisition and the violent persecution of witches were not uncommon. In my book *The Well of Remembrance,* I wrote about the karmic residues from this period that can still affect the terrors and nightmares of modern individuals and even society as a whole.

An almost entirely unacknowledged and unreconciled injustice that literally bedeviled European history for centuries is the Christian demonization and destruction of the pagan religions, which took place initially during the so-called Dark Ages and was revived in force during the Middle Ages with the persecution and extermination of several million witches. It is important to realize that there is a chasm of difference between discontinuing destructive behavior and healing and repairing the damage that has already occurred as a result of the destructive behavior. This principle holds for both the individual personal and the collective historical consciousness.

Much of the medieval church's antagonism to "witch" women was due to the women's practice of midwifery and knowledge of herbal medicine in relation to fertility, birth control, and abortion. In large part it was a battle over what we now call reproductive rights. Can we not see something of the mass hysteria of the witches' inquisition continued in the insane and fanatical violence of the abortion foes in some modern states?

Bella, as a physician-gynecologist, had studied this history intensively and was well aware of the antiwoman prejudices that have persisted into modern times. The residues of these prejudices in the conflicted abortion politics and attitudes of contemporary societies were all factors that Bella knew and confronted in her daily work. This is why she and I agreed that a targeted divination to the particular past life from which the traumatic memory fragment originated would be appropriate. She had also studied the pre-Christian religion of the Germanic people and the very different attitudes toward the power and gifts of women reflected in these myths. We decided to do a past-life memory divination with Mimir's Well of Remembrance not by drinking from the well this time, but by gazing into it. Bella had considerable clairvoyant gifts herself and identified strongly with the farseeing yet denigrated *völvas,* or seeresses, of her Germanic ancestors. Because of this and her experience, no amplifying substance was necessary or used in the following healing divination.

Divination by Gazing into the Well of Remembrance

The *Völuspa* is one of the epic Norse poems from *The Edda,* a cycle of mythic and visionary poems dating from the early Middle Ages. *Völuspa* literally means "vision songs of the völvas." The völvas were seeresses who went into ecstatic trance states to provide access to hidden knowledge of the past and future. In the *Völuspa* there are

cryptic dialogues between Odin, the knowledge-seeking god, and
an unnamed völva whom he is questioning. In the story related in
the last chapter we learned how Odin paid the price of one of his
eyes to get permission from Mimir, the wise tree giant, to drink
from the well of remembrance. In the following verse from the
poem, the völva is speaking:

Alone I sat, and outside,
as the Old One (Odin) came
and looked in my eye.
"What do you ask?
What seek you from me?
Odin, I know
where your eye is hidden:
in Mimir's marvelous well."

Here is the clue to a second divination method associated with
the well—gazing into it instead of drinking from it. Gazing into bodies of water, especially underground springs or pools in deep caves,
was a well-known method of divination in ancient times in Northern
Europe and in the Mediterranean countries. Variations of this divination practice, also known in ancient Greece, involved gazing into a
slanted mirror or a crystal ball. By gazing into a body of water, spring
or well, or a mirrored surface, you could enter a mild altered state
where you could see visions of persons or spirits and receive messages
intuitively and/or telepathically. In the *Völuspa,* the connection to
clairvoyant insight is made clear by reminding us of Odin's far-seeing
eye, which is in Mimir's well. "I know where your eye is hidden."
This means that as you gaze into the well, you would see the eye of
Odin, the god of wisdom-knowledge, looking back at you, giving you

insight and memories of the deep past. As with drinking from the well, gazing into it is also a double process—we look into the well and then reflect back on what we see.

◆ ◆ ◆

I guided Bella into the preparatory deep breathing and relaxation for the divination, lightly focusing the purifying white light-fire energy sun in the heart-center space, the head space, and the pelvic-abdominal space. She invoked her shamanic power animals and her ancestral and guiding spirits, entering into a light meditative trance state. She declared her intention and asked for help from the spirits to discover the origin of this recurring intrusive nightmare and eliminate it from her consciousness. She directed herself to sit at the roots of Mimir's world tree, having asked Mimir's permission and paid the asking price of full attention.

As she was gazing into the well I asked her to tell the story of the nightmare again, this time fully awake, as if she were watching a film sequence from a safe distance, now fortified by my presence and the presence of all her guiding spirits. I asked her to stay in the unfolding story as the screaming mob was running after her. I asked—what happens next?

I'm running up the hill, trying to escape from the screaming, shouting mob. I hear them running after me, threatening to kill me. "Hexe! Hexe!" I'm exhausted and terrified, my heart is pounding.

I asked her to stay in the terror vision—decide to stop running, turn around, and face the mob. What happens then?

I see them coming toward me and now I know I'm going to die. To my surprise, I feel calm now, although the murderous mob is still coming closer.

I reminded Bella that fear always involves anticipating that something bad or even catastrophic is about to happen. Once you accept it is happening, the fear stops. I suggested to Bella that she continue to face the raving mob as they come closer. I say, "OK, they kill you, you've accepted that. Now observe what happens as you die."

I'm floating above now, looking down at the crowd, completely free of all pain and terror. I'm entering into a warmly lighted, soothing place of peace. With great joy I see my beloved mother and aunt and grandmother, all herbalists and healers in my family, who died before me. I know some of them were also burned and killed as witches. Very much alive, they welcome me and embrace me with great rejoicing. I am home.

As Bella withdrew her downward gaze into the well of the past, she found herself firmly situated in her present life and present awareness. Not only that, her awareness had been completely raised upward into the higher dimensions, into the timeless realms above and beyond individual lifetimes, where she could meet and converse with her beloved family and ancestors. Her persecutory nightmares never returned.

❖ ❖ ❖

The stories related in the last four chapters exemplify how distorted relationship patterns carried over from a past life can manifest as karmic undercurrents in the present and how they can be healed by consciously and intentionally tuning in to that past incarnation. Although in principle reincarnation applies to the transmission of all kinds of traits and talents, both positive and negative, in my practice I have resorted to tracking past-life patterns only when present-life circumstances—including childhood, birth, familial, and prenatal factors—were insufficient to account for the difficulties experienced, and when the individual himself or herself intuitively perceived an element in his or her psyche from another lifetime.

The stories related in the following two chapters venture into the borderlands of the so-called paranormal. Possession states can be thought of with the analogy of unwanted squatters taking over a room or basement of the house of your psyche. In workshops in Europe and the United States, we have at times observed intrusive possession by malignant disembodied entities. I describe the approach we used in order to remove the possessing entity and return the identity of the individual to their own conscious control.

13

A Ceremony of Depossession from a Malignant Intrusion

Instances of apparent possession, whether by deceased humans or nonhuman entities, are not considered "real" in the worldview of contemporary psychiatry and psychology although they are recognized as natural and even common in shamanic and folk-medicine traditions around the world. In Brazil especially there is a high degree of openness even in the medical and psychological professions to traditional shamanic and nonordinary dimensions of reality in the diagnosis and treatment of physical and psychological disorders. Both harmful interference and helpful interventions by nonmaterial beings, spirits, or entities in various states and conditions are accepted as a matter of course.

There is a vast amount of literature on states of consciousness in which some other being "comes through" and speaks, or sometimes acts, through the medium of an existing personality. Such states can be arranged on a spectrum of degree of separation from the ordinary personality: from inspiration to channeling or mediumship to possession states, the most extreme dissociation.

Inspiration. Who has not had the feeling of some other energy, some other spirit, some hitherto unknown flow of positive feeling, coming through in the midst of creative activity? The thoughts and feelings of the ordinary personality are still there, but they are not in the foreground of awareness. Perhaps sometimes it is just what it seems—the spirit of another human being, whose creative work inspires us, somehow speaking/thinking in us and through us.

Channeling and Mediumism. The two terms are more or less equivalent: *mediumism* being the older term used in the nineteenth century, and *channeling* the twentieth-century version that exploded in popularity and variety in the post-1960s period in the West. The dissociative disconnect from the ordinary personality and consequent amnesia of the channeled communication is more pronounced than in simple inspiration, but it varies from person to person. Psychics or mediums may go into a more or less pronounced altered state in which their voice and mannerisms change, suggesting the presence of "someone else." Some, but not all, remember afterward what they received or "brought through" from the discarnate entity or source. Some—like Edgar Cayce—are totally dissociated in a kind of sleep trance. Cayce's channeled messages from different times, places, and lifetimes were delivered and recorded when he was completely asleep.

Possession states fall at the extreme end of the dissociative spectrum in that there is a more or less complete loss of ordinary awareness of the body and the environment. States of possession are not necessarily always pathological. Rather, they seem to occupy a kind of borderland between normality and eccentric genius. The artist

Van Gogh, for example, was known to oscillate between states of creative inspiration in which he painted masterpieces and states of madness when he needed to be confined for his own protection.

From a psychological point of view, one could regard possession as a more extreme form of obsession, which can result from an excessive emotional attachment to a vision, an idea, or to another person. For example, the creative artist, inspired by a vision, may become obsessed with the challenge of bringing the vision into his or her chosen form of expression. All of us are vulnerable to being controlled and taken over, to varying degrees, by feeling states and thought forms coming to us from others, particularly when we are in a dependency situation. Vulnerable dependencies may occur in childhood, during illness, or when there is an idealization projection toward the possessing person—whether a parent, an ancestor, or an admired older person.

Possession states involving unknown humans or even nonhuman entities are rarer than possession by deceased ancestors or relatives, but they can also occur. Occasionally my colleagues and I have seen them in medicine circles during the journeying process, possibly because in such sensitized states of consciousness the ordinary-reality defenses are partially suspended or weakened. Mild forms of partial possession may occur on longer journeys, without being recognized as such, and when the drug effect wears off, the dissociative obsession/possession may then recede into unconsciousness.

This points to a major difficulty with the possession phenomenon: a person whose consciousness is taken over by another identity does not and cannot report that this is what is taking place because the observing self has also been taken over. If the possessed person is clearly in distress or expressing destructive behavior toward self or others, some kind of depossession ritual needs to be instituted. In this and the following chapter I will relate two examples of such a situation that occurred during experiences with short-acting entheogenic substances.

◆ ◆ ◆

In my book *The Toad and the Jaguar* I described a number of individual and group sessions with an entheogenic medicine we symbolically called "Jaguar," and whose scientific name is *5-methoxy-dimethyltryptamine,* or *5-meo-DMT* for short. In the book I relate my findings from more than thirty years of experiences and observations with this substance in various groups and individuals, both in Europe and in the United States. This substance, like its better-known chemical relative DMT, can be smoked or inhaled in a vaporizer pipe, producing an experience that lasts about ten to fifteen minutes, with the intensity dependent on the dosage. But unlike DMT, 5-meo-DMT can also be ingested through the nasal passages as a snuff, not a smoke. Various plant sources of 5-meo-DMT are in fact taken as snuff preparations by several different indigenous South American tribes. When taken intranasally in this way, the experience can, dependent on dosage, induce a heightened state of consciousness lasting about fifty to sixty minutes.

The snuffing mode of ingesting of this compound is particularly suitable for the methodical and productive exploration of heightened states. The dosage ingested can be more precisely calibrated than with the smoking method, and the one-hour duration lends itself to systematic observations while experiences lasting a few minutes do not. Among the experiences that I relate in *The Toad and the Jaguar* are experiences with possession states and with depossession procedures that we improvised to deal with them.

Possession states were, in my experience with groups and individuals, extremely rare. Of course I have no way of knowing how often they occur in the general population of individuals that use these substances, especially since possession states may often not be recognized as such. I want to emphasize that I do not consider possession states a function of this specific medicine, or a kind of "drug effect." In the next chapter I will relate possession experiences with a different medicine. The main therapeutic advantage of working with 5-meo-DMT is that the specific drug action is relatively brief, so that the therapeutic depossession project can be more clearly implemented—and repeated, if necessary.

◆ ◆ ◆

A group of twelve participants met in Switzerland in the southern foothills of the Alps for a week of entheogenic explorations with different medicines. We were in a large house on a lake, and for our journeys we used two rooms: an outer room and an inner room. The outer room was more or less square in shape and was where we sat in chairs in a circle and did our preparatory discussions, meditations, and declarations of intentions. We created an altar in the middle of the room, and everyone placed their personal ritual object on it at the beginning of the ceremony, with invocations of the ancestors and guiding spirits. After the preparation the group would walk for the amplified journey sessions into an inner rectangular meeting room, set up with two rows of mattresses on which people would lie, within arm's length of one another, and a narrow central corridor. We called this set-up our "spirit canoe" or "spirit raft." The size of the room did not allow us to lie in a circle for the actual inner journeys.

My friend Martin, a Jungian psychotherapist, and I sat at opposite ends of the canoe, guiding it through the "in between" realms of consciousness and spirit, while the two rows of travelers alternated between sitting facing the center of the room or lying down with their heads toward the center. Martin and I had evolved this format for our sessions over the twenty years we worked together in that space. After the deep inner medicine journeys, we would always walk in procession back to the outer room, where we sat in our chairs around the altar in the middle and did our closing rituals and prayers.

In my book *Allies for Awakening* I describe in some detail the various elements of entheogenic group ceremonies, including the circle structure, the council format, the ceremonial altar, the talking stick, and others. A unique feature of the setup described for our ceremonies in the Alps was this migrating from the outer room to the inner and then back again at the end of the ceremony. We used to say, respectfully in a joking manner, that the outer room where we first met and prepared ourselves was like the vagina of the Earth Mother, and the inner room where we met to dive down deep to be reborn was her womb.

◆ ◆ ◆

During a group ceremony with the Jaguar snuff medicine a woman I shall call Bertha went into a dissociated state. She seemed oblivious to the others around her, and her movements became increasingly violent. She was thrashing her whole body and arms from side to side and breathing audibly, in obvious distress. Everyone's eyes were covered with eye shades, but her neighbors on the mats, obviously aware of her movements, were cautiously moving farther away.

She did return to her normal state of consciousness along with everyone else, as the intensity of the medicine effect waned, after about forty to sixty minutes. She was badly shaken by the experience. She said that subjectively she felt that she had been abducted by flying alien beings who were operating on her brain, for some purpose she could not fathom and in a process over which she had no choice or control. After returning to the normal waking state she participated normally in conversations and the evening meal, although her mood was obviously subdued.

The following day, after extensive discussions and at her request, we arranged a separate session for Bertha for the explicit purpose of exorcising this apparent demonic intrusion. She would be the only one taking the medicine—at a much lower, just above threshold, dose. All the others would simply be present and supportive in a meditative state, without any additional medicine. Her instructions were to concentrate on staying completely present in her body and aware of her environment the whole time. She was to prevent dissociation by focusing her attention on breathing and on the purifying light-fire meditation process in the central vertical axis and throughout the energy field. All of us practiced the same method, each one holding steady with mindful here-now awareness.

One of the men in the group, a friend of hers, was seated on her right dynamic side and was instructed to magnetically draw toxic energy from her, burning it up in the consuming fire of his energy field. A woman friend was seated on her left side and was guided to pour loving, healing energy into her left, receptive side. Another friend was seated at her feet and was instructed to draw energy downward to drain out toxic residues, while keeping her grounded in the feet. I sat at her head, holding the space around her head with my hands. I had learned these kinds of group depossession rituals from observing and participating in Brazilian spiritist ceremonies known as *Umbanda* and *Barquinia*. We listened to a low-volume recording of simple drumming and made low continuous humming sounds to accompany it.

All of us, including Bertha, invoked the guiding, protective, and healing spirits, animal and human, with which we were connected. The intention we held was to help Bertha rid herself of the unwanted intrusions. Speaking directly into her ears, I asked Bertha to call on the intrusive flying spirits from the previous day to show themselves, identify themselves, and state what they wanted. Bertha replied in a low, frightened voice: "They say they want my energy."

I then spoke to them through her, in a loud emphatic voice: "Bertha's energy is hers, not yours. You have no right to hang on to her. You must leave immediately." I also made a verbal request, which was reinforced with the group's silent prayers, for the assembled light spirits working with us to take the intruders away. Several of us could perceive fibrous threads that seemed to be implanted or attached to Bertha's head, and we focused intention and attention on drawing these implanted threads out and burning them up, thereby purifying the subtle energy field. Over the next twenty to thirty minutes of this process the space and field around her body seemed to become lighter and less dense. She said she felt lighter, in the sense of less heavy and pulled downward, and that the intrusive spirits seemed to have left. All of us, including Bertha, recognized that we could not know whether the intrusive spirits would stay away or whether they could return.

Bertha told us that she had had a fear of being left alone since childhood, and she recognized that this fear functioned as an "open door" to intrusive entities or spirits. Questioning revealed that this fear had first come up when she was four years old and her beloved grandfather had suddenly died. She was traumatized by that loss and felt abandoned. We know from accounts by researchers like Adam Crabtree, related in his book *Multiple Man: Explorations in Possession and Multiple Personality,* that children who have lost parents or other important protectors or who are in a vulnerable state due to illness and hospitalization are particularly susceptible to being taken over by spirits of deceased people. The possessing "entities" in the majority of cases are typically family members who have not reconciled themselves to being dead and may latch onto a vulnerable child's mind.

Bertha had been advised by her counselor not to participate in experiments with mind-expanding substances because of her psychic vulnerability—something she had not told us. After this experience she followed her counselor's advice, stopped using entheogens and focused on practices for strengthening her boundaries and raising her self-esteem.

14

Converting a Possessing Entity into a Protective Ally

Marvin, a psychiatrist and friend of mine, sought my help because he was experiencing episodes of being taken over, involuntarily, by a malevolent spirit or entity during group sessions in which plant entheogens were used. The self-directed group, in which I also participated sometimes, consisted of physicians and psychologists exploring and testing the healing potentials of entheogens, in particular a medicine called *jurema,* a concoction of two plants similar in its effects to *ayahuasca.* Participants in this group would sit or lie in a circle and use a talking staff to share their stories or songs. In my book *Allies for Awakening,* I describe such self-organizing egalitarian groups where there is no one particular individual with greater experience who is the recognized guide. Instead, the group leadership functions are rotated or shared among different individuals. The following passages are from that book (pages 66–69).

In self-organizing, egalitarian groups there is great variation in the time and attention devoted to preparatory ritual elements such as prayers or spirit invocations and explicit statements of intentions. My informal observations suggest that the more attention that is paid to these preparatory elements the more productive and satisfying the rituals are likely to be. Furthermore, in groups consisting of friends whose ordinary lives include interactions with each other and their families, it can be a helpful preparatory practice to clear the air of any unresolved disagreements and exchange apologies as needed so that lingering negativity does not infect the spirit of the inner journey.

In such egalitarian groups with rotating functions, there is usually a sharing of responsibilities, similar to the peyote circle gatherings. One person or family provides the place for the ceremony, which is typically held at night and is followed by sleep in the same place and some kind of integrative process and food sharing, either after the ceremony or sometimes the next morning. There is explicit and/or tacit agreement on the main elements: people sit and lie in chosen places, often in an approximate circle, which allows everyone to see everyone equally; someone brings and administers the chosen medicine, which is dispensed and ingested (drunk, eaten, injected, smoked, or snuffed); someone provides the music, either recorded or live, or both; and some variation of a talking stick ritual is used for periodic sharing of experiences. Three of these elements deserve special and careful consideration—the *dosing,* the *music,* and the *talking stick rounds.*

The dispensing of the initial medicine is a pretty straightforward process, but the timing and dispensing of *booster doses* can make a big difference between productive and inharmonious sessions. Booster doses typically extend the length of the action of the medicine in the body-mind. Thus if there is at-will taking of additional booster doses it will be that much more difficult to perform a closing ceremony after which most everyone moves to the different time-space mode of socializing and eating. Therefore experience and common sense suggest that there be one pre-agreed time after the initial dose, let's say roughly 1 hour, where a supplemental or booster dose is ingested by those who choose to, but not thereafter.

In the section of this book [*Allies for Awakening*] on *Spiritual Medicine Practices* I discuss the dose-related issues and the all-important distinction between the *effective dose* and the *dissociative dose.* To my mind, it is an important part of taking responsibility for one's own health and well-being, as well as consideration for others in a group ceremony and the larger community, that the individual be aware of and calibrate his or her own intake of these mind-expanding substances with sensitivity to these factors. For this reason also, I personally think that it is best if the dispensing of medicines and booster doses is carried out by one individual in the group who has chosen to either abstain altogether from taking any medicines or only takes a threshold amount, so that his or her normal judgment is not impaired. I have been in non-directed, leaderless groups where the choosing and taking of booster doses was at will, by people with obviously impaired judging functions—with resulting effects both unpleasant and unproductive of useful inner work.

What music is played, live or recorded and by whom, can also be a source of disagreements and distractions if not carefully planned. In the NAC [Native American Church] peyote ceremonies there is one drummer who sees to the timing and structure of the ceremony and also supports individual singers. The contemporary self-directed, leaderless groups in which I have been a participant-observer have also usually had one person (by rotation or agreement) organize the selection of recorded music to be played. If all agree that this person will select the recordings for this particular session, then this avoids pointless and distracting disagreements about whether other music would be preferable at any given moment. When I have been in groups like that and the music played was something I didn't particularly "like," I used the opportunity to practice the Taoist mantra "for those who have no preferences for or against anything, the Way is as wide open as the World." In time the music was changed to a different mode and my mood changed accordingly. So this is the advantage of leaving the selection of recordings to be played to one person in the ceremony, by agreement. (Metzner 2015, 66–69)

◆ ◆ ◆

At the time of Marvin's request, the group of friends and colleagues working with jurema adhered to a circle structure, with people either sitting or lying with their heads to the center. They placed personally significant objects on an altar, and they did a preparatory round of sharing, bringing each other up to date on changes in their lives and clearing the air of any residual misunderstandings. They also used a talking staff or crystal for periodic rounds of sharing either spoken words or chanting, and they had one person sequence the music selections, which were accepted without resistance.

However, at the time this group had a rather loose structure that permitted free talking and interaction among the participants.

I personally found this structure insufficiently protective and too chaotic for useful inner work. In my experience the ceremonies that are most productive of insights and learning are those in which ordinary back-and-forth conversation is completely absent from the beginning to the end of the ceremony, and both of those transitions are intentionally marked and observed. With agreed adherence to such ritual form, it appears that the experience can remain in the more holistic right-brain mode of awareness and only return to left-brain thinking and talking mode at the end of the ceremony. Although I participated in this particular group's circles sometimes, at other times I declined or left early when it was safe to do so, having taken only a minimal dose. I was in fact present in at least one of the sessions in which Marvin became increasingly possessed, although neither he himself nor any of the other participants, myself included, knew what was happening with him.

◆ ◆ ◆

Marvin told me in private conversation later that during a number of these group sessions over the course of a several months he found himself being *taken over* by what appeared to be a malevolent entity in the form of a jaguar, which he had originally thought of as a healing ally. One time he nearly bit another circle participant in the neck, while following an inner prompting that indicated to him that his biting was supposedly healing the other man. He told me later that during these group sessions he would go into a kind of empty hell space, where he would hear a malevolent voice communicating that it was going to destroy him.

For several weeks he felt "out of sorts," and he exploded at his partner at home and at his colleagues at work, which was uncharacteristic of him. He observed that even his dog seemed to be afraid of him, avoiding him when he came home rather than greeting him with his usual tail-wagging enthusiasm. He became afraid that something in his psychological work on himself, or in his makeup, was inviting malevolent possession, possibly driving him insane. Of course there was nothing in his medical/psychiatric worldview that accommodated the notion of possession, but he knew of my interest and experience in the area. We decided to create a depossession or exorcism ritual—and this time without any entheogenic amplification.

In his capacity as an emergency room psychiatrist, Marvin had encountered a young woman with a perplexing psychiatric history. She was hospitalized at the unit in which he worked due to sudden outbursts of extreme violence in which she severely injured other people or herself. Self-injury included fracturing her own bones. Between episodes, which appeared to be completely unprovoked, she was a sweet, petite young woman whose behavior, mannerisms, speech, and thinking seemed entirely normal.

Diagnostically, she was an enigma, Marvin told me, even after months on the psychiatric unit. She did not meet the criteria for psychotic illness or bipolar disorder, and medical workups to evaluate her for seizure or other neurological disorders revealed nothing that could explain her behavior. She continued to have sudden episodes of profoundly disturbing violence, and a number of the hospital staff members were injured. Medications seemed to be of almost no benefit, and at times she required physical restraint. One day a nurse commented that if ever she had encountered a case of possession, this was it.

In his letter to me, Marvin related the following experience that occurred in the group circle:

I began to hear what I can only describe as "malevolent intonations."
It clearly sounded like language, although none that I had ever heard,
and the energy was chillingly malevolent. I felt as though I was under
attack and I responded by psychologically "hunkering down." I don't
have a clear memory of what followed. Other circle members tell me
there was a period in which I thrashed about on the floor and was
completely internally focused so that no communication with them
was possible. I have fragments of memories in which I felt as though
I was in some kind of epic battle, and at times spirit energies seemed
to come into my body. One of these was Jaguar, a personal totem,
which I remember filling my body, being present for moments in
the room, and then leaving. Eventually, I started to regain normal
consciousness, but I felt tired and out of sorts.

The experience was certainly not what I had previously
experienced with this medicine. The next day I went home, still
feeling off. When I got home, I was puzzled by the behavior of my
dog, with whom I was very close. Normally, he would greet me
with enthusiastic affection, as though I had been gone for months,
but on this day he seemed reserved and would not get near me.
Over the course of the next few weeks, I came to recognize that
I was out of sorts with virtually everyone in my life. There was
uncharacteristic tension between my brother and me, with my
wife, and at work. My coworkers, who were used to my usually
calm demeanor, commented that I seemed bothered or upset. And
strangely, my dog continued to avoid me.

I began to wonder what was going on and had to ask myself if
I was going crazy. It was just so weird, how suddenly everything had
shifted, and all of my relationships, even with my dog, had soured.
I continued to work on the psychiatric unit, including treating the
young woman mentioned above who continued to have paroxysms

of violence. I was vaguely aware of feeling tense and irritable and could tell that I responded to people and circumstances in an uncharacteristic manner, but I had no idea how to think about this.

One day, about three weeks after the medicine circle, I was home alone, soaking in my hot tub. I was reflecting on the matters I'm describing, and candidly, I was really beginning to wonder if I was losing it. Suddenly, I became aware of the same malevolent energy that had been intoning at the medicine circle. I don't recall actually hearing the intonations this time, but I clearly recognized that the same energy that had been the source of those sounds was present with me this day, as I sat in the hot tub. Immediately, I knew what needed to be done. I very directly gave my attention to this presence, and once it was fixed in my awareness, I said with great authority, "You're not welcome here. Leave!"

What I experienced next was an immediate sense of something lifting off of me. I felt light and suddenly unburdened. And I realized that I now felt alone in a way I had not been feeling the previous weeks. This evoked a dawning realization and an extraordinarily creepy feeling that I had been raped. I felt disgust and revulsion and a deep sense of having been profoundly violated. I was at a loss about how to think about this. As a psychiatrist, this all seemed very crazy, but I had to acknowledge that the most intellectually honest response was to recognize that, whatever they meant, these were my experiences.

Over the next few days, Marvin quickly saw that, with regard to relationships, things were back to normal. His wife and coworkers commented on this, and his dog was back to expressing his usual unbridled affection. What was also back to normal was the behavior of the young woman he had been treating. All of the violent episodes had stopped. In one week, after months on the unit, and with no change in her medications, she was able to be discharged. He was told later by a coworker who still worked in the department that she had never returned to the hospital with another of her episodes.

◆ ◆ ◆

Although the particular situation of possession by the self-destructive young woman had been resolved, Marvin asked me to assist him in clearing whatever residual tendencies or patterns in his makeup had led to him being vulnerable to this kind of takeover and to coach him in methods to avoid them in the future. I started by "smudging" the space with sage, brushing him down with a feather fan in the front and back and on the left and right sides, and invoking all the protective spirits we both knew. He especially invoked his animal spirit allies for their help in dealing with his malevolent entity. Crystals were placed in the four directions of the room to add clarity and protective focus to the space and the process. We were both in a light meditative trance, focused but without amplifying substance.

I then directed Marvin in the light-fire yogic practice of activating the Three Rings of Shiva to protect and energize the energy field. In this practice, one ring of light-fire energy, as shown in the usual Shiva statues, encircles the field in the vertical upper-lower, left-right plane; a second ring encircles the field in the horizontal front-back, left-right plane; and the third encircles the field in the vertical upper-lower, front-back plane. The three rings of light-fire serve to strongly define, balance, and protect the energy field from inner or outer disturbances.

After practicing this process for a while I asked Marvin if he noticed anything. He replied, "I see a brownish mass in the left-front quarter sphere." The left side is the receptive side of the energy field. Evidently something dark both in color and in psychic "feel" had intruded into his field and lodged there. I suggested to Marvin that he focus on this mass and ask to see it more clearly. He then said that a part of the mass had peeled off like a mask revealing a face, brown skinned, with green eyes. It reminded him of two different African spirits or entities he had encountered before. I directed Marvin to ask the being or entity behind the mask some questions:

QUESTION: "Is this connected to the possessing entity?"
ANSWER: "Yes."

QUESTION: "What does it want?"
ANSWER: "It wants to feed on me."

QUESTION: "Where is it from?"
ANSWER: "A whole group or network is behind it."

Marvin and I both sensed that we knew enough to recognize this as an intruding entity, akin to an uninvited squatter taking up residence in your house and eating your food supplies. I blew smoke from tobacco, which is universally recognized in shamanic culture as a powerful warrior plant, all around his body on all sides, as well as smudging again with sage. I also used the feather fan and rattle all around him on every side, head to feet. Together we held the possessing entity with light-fire from all directions and, supported by both our allies and spirit guides, we explicitly and loudly demanded that it leave.

Marvin then reported that the entity had turned into a snake and moved into his belly, where it was producing fear. He noted that it evidently fed on the fear it produces in the humans it invades. It started to devour him from inside. Trying to pull it out of his body seemed endless. He mentioned that he had had frightening kundalini-type experiences as a teenager and surmised that the fear had attracted the alien energy at that time.

I said: "Call on your own divine serpent energy to counter this entity, merging with the negative snake. Allow your own divine serpent energy to rise upward from the belly toward the heart field and then on upward to the throat and head. This protective divine serpent will then overshadow the crown of the head. Invoke the image of the Buddha meditating with an umbrella of protective cobras over his head." Practicing in this way for several minutes the negative, hungry snake eventually left. The wise, protective serpent remained as a spirit ally.

In a subsequent session with Marvin, I showed him a further specific practice of raising the serpent energy, using the image of the staff of Asclepius, the ancient Greek god of healing. The Asclepius staff consists of one serpent coiling up around a central staff. Since Marvin was by profession a physician, this was a practice totally attuned to his life work. The central staff can be seen as an emblem of the central vertical axis, associated with the cerebrospinal axis between the crown of the head and the pelvic floor. The serpent coiling from side to side represents the *vagus* ("wandering") nerve, which winds from side to side connecting the nerves and other organs in the pelvic cauldron with those in the heart and feeling center and those in the head and thinking center.

When the serpentine energies of sexuality and power normally focused in the lower parts of the body are disconnected from the emotional, mental, and spiritual centers in the upper body, they are vulnerable to being taken over by random destructive external stimuli. This is the basis for yogic practices, such as "raising the kundalini," designed to turn the potentially poisonous snake energy into creative and transformative energy. Similarly, in the life story of the Buddha, we hear of the many-headed cobra that spread its hoods over the sitting meditator, protecting him from the assaults of demonic and destructive forces.

The practice of raising serpentine energy is also conveyed in the popular Indian folkloric image of the flute-playing snake charmer, raising the cobra upright out of the basket. The snake is charmed and hypnotized not so much by the sound of the flute, but by the side-to-side movements of the flute player. I showed Marvin how to use the yogic practice known as the *snake-charmer mudra,* in which one moves the head and torso from side to side in slow serpentine movements, synchronized with breathing. This movement activates and harmonizes the upper and lower parts of your body, bringing balance and vitality into body, heart, and mind integrated by Spirit. Humming and toning could be added to the mix of practices that can function to let the sinuous serpentine energy currents move harmoniously and peacefully through the body. With these inner shields and practices, Marvin felt that he had enough tools and the confidence to protect himself in his practices as a healer and explorer of consciousness.

15

The Healing Wisdom
of the Serpent

Western participants in ayahuasca ceremonies often report powerful healing and visionary experiences with serpent imagery, which is also portrayed in the art inspired by ayahuasca. In his breakthrough integration of modern science with shamanic knowledge systems, *The Cosmic Serpent,* Jeremy Narby proposed that the DNA molecule, which has the form of a double helix, might be the molecular counterpart to the hallucinated serpents of ayahuasca visions. "Not only among Amazonian shamans, but throughout the world, in Asia, the Mediterranean, Australia, serpent images are used to represent the basic life force and regarded as a source of knowledge—the wisdom of the serpent" (Narby 1998, 29–30).

While the DNA double helix may well be the source of serpent visions in ayahuasca at the molecular level, another source at the ordinary botanical level could be that the ayahuasca potion is a concoction of the bark of the snakelike vine *Banisteriopsis caapi* and the leafy DMT-containing plant *Psychotria viridis.* Snakes and serpentine forms are frequently, if not universally, encountered in ayahuasca experiences. In the anthology of ayahuasca studies that I compiled, *The Ayahuasca Experience,* four or five of the twenty-five or so experience accounts mention serpent imagery, including my own.

When I started to work with ayahuasca myself I had ample opportunity to experience the healing and visionary power of this Amazonian hallucinogenic plant concoction and its serpentine connections. Here is an account of my introduction to the ayahuasca serpents from an experience I had with my friend Terence McKenna, when I was in my fifties.

> There were shapes and images of plants, animals, humans, ethereal temples and cities, flying craft, and floating structures. Particular images would emerge from the continuous flux and then be absorbed back into it. As the images of forms and objects receded back into the swaying fabric of visions, I realized I was seeing them as if projected on the twisting coils of an enormous serpent with glittering silvery and green designs on its skin. I could not see either the head or the tail of the serpent, which gave me a rough sense of its size: it encompassed the entire two-story building. Curiously, the sight of this gigantic serpent did not evoke the slightest fear; on the contrary, my emotional response was one of awe and humility at the magnificence of this being and its spiritual power. I was reminded of Pablo Amaringo's ayahuasca paintings, which depict the giant serpent seen in the visions as the "mother spirit," on which smaller spirits can ride and travel through the world. In the Amazonian shamanic worldview they recognize three different serpent *mamas*—of the air, of the river, and of the forest. In my experience, which took place in Northern California, there seemed to be one gigantic

serpent mother, coiling and rippling through the entire length and breadth of the valley in which we were situated.

Then I met another serpent in my visions, more "normal" in its dimensions: in fact it was about the same size as me. It entered my body through my mouth and started to slowly wind its way through my stomach and intestines over the next two or three hours. When it got to the gut, there was some cramping, and incredibly loud sounds of gurgling and digesting were coming from my viscera. I became aware of the morphic resonance between a serpent and the intestines: the form of the snake is more or less a long intestinal tract, with a head end at the mouth and tail end at the anus . . . The gut is serpentine, with its twists and coils and its peristaltic movement. So the serpent, in winding its way through my intestinal tract was "teaching" my intestines how to be more powerful and effective. (Metzner 2014, 120–21)

In a dream vision I had sometime after this first experience, I began to realize that there are basically these two kinds of biophysical serpentine structures in the body: one is the intestinal gut serpent, coiling and winding through the abdomen from the mouth to the anus. Connected with the oldest evolutionary layer of the brain, the intestinal serpent functions to break down ingested food stuff and to excrete and purge waste matter. The other serpentine structure in the human body is the pair of electromagnetic energy currents moving up, across, and along the central axis. In the symbolic terminology of the Indian system of tantra yoga, there are said to be two channels through which the kundalini energy with its twin serpentine currents rises upward, coiling around the central axis: a solar current (*pingala*) and a lunar current (*ida*). Intentionally and consciously balancing these is a central practice of this tradition.

It is interesting to reflect on the fact that the perceptions, during an ayahuasca experience, of these seemingly outrageously intimate intrusions into our deepest guts, including sometimes massive purging without feeling sick or if so only temporarily, are being mediated by the brain stem and the enteric nervous system, the network of 100 million neurons lining the inside and outside of the intestines. This enteric nerve network and the associated brain stem is the oldest layer of the brain in evolutionary terms, the brain that we share with our reptilian ancestors. Reptilian consciousness is nonsymbolic and nonemotional but involves deep primal sensing. One of the meanings of the "raising the serpent" metaphor alludes to connecting the deep primal sensing of the reptilian brain stem with the more evolved kind of awareness in the limbic system associated with mammals, and the human symbolic understandings mediated in the cortical layers.

After I had been working with ayahuasca for several years and had also been experiencing guided prenatal regression therapy, without medicines, I recognized yet another aspect of these many-layered memory circuits. The experience of being completely surrounded or contained in the coils of a gigantic moving serpent—of which you can't see the head or the tail and that is "as big as the house you're in"—could be a somatic memory of the prenatal fetus, who resides in the maternal womb surrounded by the mother's coiling, peristaltic intestines. The Amazonian shamans say, "The mother of ayahuasca is a snake." This is the giant mother serpent that provides both shelter and nourishment as well as information about the world through the telepathic rapport between the mother and fetus.

An experience with entheogenic or visionary substances is always a function of several interacting factors: the specific medicine ingested, the set or intention or purpose of the "trip," the personal history of the individual, and the setting or ritual context of the experience. The following account describes the experience of a woman in an ayahuasca ceremony that was focused on healing and divination but not necessarily on serpentine imagery. She brought to the experience her own meditation experiences with Shiva the Hindu god of yogis, who is usually represented in paintings and bronze sculptures with serpents coiling around his shoulders and in his hair.

About twenty minutes into the journey I saw an image of the ayahuasca vine and then the most amazing thing happened. I was practicing staying centered in my heart, not my head, as it was a vital point of the divination. To help me focus I placed my hands over my heart center and continuously said a silent mantra, "Shiva in my heart, Shiva in my heart." After concentrating on that for some minutes the visions began in earnest and it was more than a vision because I felt it so strongly. A king cobra rose up from the base of my spine and upward, expanding its hood like an umbrella over my head, protecting me. The cobra was beautiful with amber and gold colors, and its pink tongue tickled my face off and on during the night. I felt happy and balanced. When I asked the cobra, "How long will you stay?" he answered, "I have always been with you and now that you are aware of me I will be able to be more present in your life." He said that when I opened my eyes I would be looking out of his eyes. He was very stern and yet compassionate.

The cobra pointed out to me the muscular armoring on my shoulders. I have experienced chronic pain in my shoulders and neck for many years. I saw that the armor was beautifully carved and pounded with intricate patterns. I had had it for so long that I made a real art piece of it! I realized it had to do with family responsibilities that I took on at age seven and continued to carry for the next forty years. I visualized myself taking off the armor and giving it to Shiva who was standing at my feet. It felt good and I had considerable relief from the shoulder pain.

Serpent Visions with Magic Mushrooms

Although serpentine visions are perhaps more often experienced and associated with ayahuasca, they are by no means absent with other hallucinogens, as in the following story of an experience with psilocybe mushrooms. This woman's account is from my edited anthology *Sacred Mushroom of Visions—Teonanácatl.*

I heard the mushroom beings' friendly voices greeting me, welcoming me, calling me "Little Sister." It felt wonderful, like coming home. I entered their world. They took me to a rainforest where everything was magnificently alive and vibrant. The roots spiraled like snakes in the rich fecund Earth. The roots became snakes, *everything* became snakes, as I heard her say, "I am Mama Quilla," who is a South American moon goddess. I saw the radiant full moon illuminating a tree where a beautiful white plumed bird roosted in the upper branches and snakes coiled like roots at the base of the trunk. This was her manifestation. Then I became her; I *was* her. I felt myself embody this form, energy, and vision. Colorful, vividly patterned snakes, like pythons, were coiling within me. My body was completely made from this serpent energy that was winding, undulating, spiraling, slithering in an ecstatic dance within each cell. I just sat there in wonder. . . .

Then the mushrooms began to speak again. They were giggling and said: "Unless you get by the snakes, we won't tell you any more secrets." I knew they were telling me about the snakes being guardians of the mysteries. I felt completely united with all of nature, the Goddess, the land, all of life. I understood that the mushroom beings are guardians of the Earth and that through our communion with them we learn to protect the well-being of the land. They showed me awesome realms of pure beauty. Everything seemed so simple in the quiet stillness of the luminous indigo desert night. . . . I realized a profound union with a global lineage of serpent priestesses, the *pythia,* oracular protectors of the Earth. I saw how I was part of an ancient lineage through time and place. . . . I was then given personal guidance about my children and the future. It was like visiting with the Grandmothers, I felt so much at home. . . . The snakes were my adornments, my jewelry, symbols of this oracular power of the Earth to speak through her priestesses. (Metzner 2005, 195)

Kundalini: Serpent Power in Indian Yoga

Kundalini (Sanskrit for "the coiled one") is associated with the experience and the practice of an energy current rising up and energizing the chakras, from the *muladhara* (root chakra) at the base of the spine to the *sahasrara* (crown chakra) at the top of the head. In the literature of the Indian yoga traditions, *kundalini* is the symbolic name of this fiery yet fluid psychophysical energy lying dormant like a coiled snake in the root chakra at the base of the central axis. The serpent symbolizes generative and regenerative energy, which is usually expended and expressed outwardly in sexual activity but can be "raised up" internally through breathing and concentrative practices in a kind of transmutation of the energy. Thus the serpent fire of kundalini is said to rise vertically upward through the body, like the snake rising from its coiled position in response to the hypnotic sounds of the snake charmer.

Through the intentional practice of kundalini yoga, the fiery energy is said to move upward through the body's energy centers, energizing them and burning off the "coverings" that block their functioning. This so-called raising of the kundalini can lead to problems if it is not preceded by purification practices to reduce tensions and blockages of energy. As it rises up through the body's energy centers, the balanced serpentine energy currents are said to promote healing and longevity. At the level of the throat center, they stimulate the vocal apparatus for singing, speech, and creative expression. Raised all the way to the crown center at the top of the head, this energy can be transmuted to a spiritual transcendence, associated with out-of-body trance experience. In the classic meditation posture, as seen in the iconic image of the Buddha sitting with hands folded, the two energy channels are in calm and centered balance. The body is motionless, but not asleep. Attention is focused on inward contemplation.

There is a vast literature on the yogic breathing and concentrative practices designed to raise serpentine kundalini energy up through the chakras. In the energy-flow meditation practices that I was taught in my ten-year immersion in a Western school of *agni yoga* ("yoga of fire"), the focus is not so much on raising the energy upward, from the root chakra to the crown of the head, but rather to bring higher-frequency subtle energies down from the spiritual dimensions, spreading and grounding them throughout the physical body and limbs, from top to toe and deeply into every organ and cell of the body.

In practical terms, instead of focusing only on the chakras, I have come to prefer working with a threefold division of the body and energy field, each of which contains three or four of the traditional yogic energy centers. This is basically similar to the practice found in the teachings of Chinese Taoism, with its three basic *t'an tien*, or "elixir fields." The energy currents can flow downward from above, or upward from below, or both downward and upward from the middle, and in coiling patterns. In the following I describe the experiences with three different serpentine symbols in which the "serpents" were practiced as inner yogic energy currents.

Ouroboros, Caduceus, Asclepius

The following are the three serpentine emblems or symbols that we practiced as inner processes.

Ouroboros

The *ouroboros* (Greek for "tail-eating snake") is shown in medieval alchemical illustrations as a serpent with its tail in its mouth. "Here is the Dragon that devours its own tail" is the caption for a seventeenth-century image that symbolically depicts this energy current that runs around the vertical axis of the body, integrating and balancing the three essence fields. There is an interesting correspondence to this ouroboros circuit in the Chinese acupuncture system, where we have a yang current and a yin current meeting at the upper lip, just where the dragon has its tail in its mouth. See the illustration on page 154.

Caduceus

The *caduceus* (Greek for "herald's staff") consists of a vertical staff with two serpents winding around it (see the illustration on page 155). The tails of the serpents are in the generative organs. They cross over the vertical axis at the abdomen, the heart, and the head, with the winged heads of the serpents meeting at the top of the

Working with the Ouroboros Energy Circuit
(and acupuncture channels)

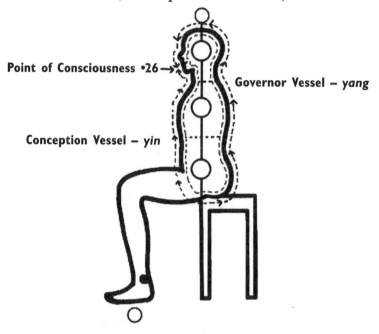

Point of Consciousness •26 →

Governor Vessel – *yang*

Conception Vessel – *yin*

"Here is the Dragon that devours its own tail."
Atalanta fugiens, 1648
by Michael Maier

Comparison of the central energy currents—*Governor Vessel* and
Conception Vessel—of the Chinese acupuncture system with the European
alchemical image of the *ouroboros* serpent with its tail in its mouth.

head. The caduceus is also called the "Hermes staff," associated with Hermes the messenger deity, who is sometimes shown in sculptures and paintings with wings at his feet and his head, carrying the staff.

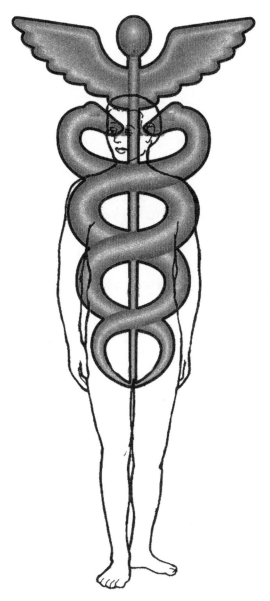

The caduceus, associated with heralds and messengers, superimposed on the body, depicting esoteric serpentine energy currents.

In Greek myth Hermes is the messenger of the high gods, carrying messages from the higher dimensions above to the human, earthly world below and vice versa. In ancient and medieval European culture he is associated with heralds and messengers in general, and also, paradoxically, with liars, gamblers, and thieves. Perhaps the meaning behind his association with liars and thieves is to emphasize his role as the inner voice that reminds the miscreant of the promptings of his conscience.

Staff of Asclepius

In modern Western culture, particularly in the United States, the caduceus with two serpents is sometimes associated with the medical and pharmaceutical professions, as an emblem. But this association is a mistake. The staff of Asclepius, the Greek god of healing, is a staff with *one snake* coiling around it (see the illustration on page 157). In ancient Greece, Asclepius was the healer deity who presided over the underground caves with healing waters, where the sick came to have their healing sleep, while the sacred serpents slithered around their bodies at night. The daughter of Asclepius, who assisted in the healing work, was Hygeia, from whose name we derive the concepts and practices of hygiene.

◆ ◆ ◆

These three mythic serpent images from the Western esoteric tradition have lost their association with particular practices and are generally thought of as purely symbolic. In dictionaries of symbols, one can read of serpents as symbols life force or of sexuality and regenerative power. Serpent symbolism may also be expressed in sinuous movements of dance and other arts.

But the following experiences in contemporary individuals show that in fact these symbolic serpents are connected with specific inner healing practices dating back to the ancient Greek civilization. The external symbolism that encoded the practice has remained through

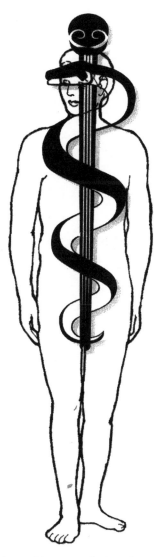

The staff of Asclepius, with one coiled snake, is the image properly associated with the medical profession. It depicts the esoteric energy current associated with the vagus nerve.

modern times but without the awareness of the inner, esoteric practice. In the practice the serpent imagery is internalized. It is perceived as currents of life energy flowing in specific patterns inside the body while the outer-body-and-personality form of the person is sitting in quiet meditation posture.

The vertical staff found in all the serpent symbols and emblems depicts the vertical energy axis of the human body, and the single or double serpents winding around it refer to the sinuous energy currents flowing around the axis. The single snake, such as the one on the Asclepius staff, can be seen as a symbolic representation of the current flow through the vagus nerve, which, along with many small branches, has one main single nerve fiber that runs from the generative organs (testes and ovaries), winding back and forth across the central axis, and up to the crown of the head. Since the vagus nerve extends from the sacral base of the pelvic organs to the brain stem and limbic system, we can see how practices associated with the Asclepius serpent could play a key role in the healing integration of the three main chambers of the body's energy systems.

Serpentine Healings and Teachings with Amplification by 5-Meo-DMT

All the following experiences occurred in a series of sessions I conducted, many years ago, with 5-meo-DMT ingested intranasally as a snuff powder. The preparation consisted of some hatha yoga postures, gentle breathing practices, and agni yoga meditations with inner light-fire concentrated in the head center, heart center, and abdominal-pelvic centers. I then described and guided a practice session with the three serpentine meditations. Participants were encouraged to choose whichever one they resonated with the most to practice again with the amplification provided by the snuff medicine.

In our sessions, the 5-meo-DMT was drawn into the nostrils with a straw at a threshold dose of 5 mg, which needs to be carefully measured since it cannot be accurately estimated with mere eyeball inspection. The effective threshold dose of this medicine is 5 mg, and the dissociative dose, at which half the subjects tend to space out, although they are not harmed, is only 15 mg—a very narrow range. While in the relaxed and mindful state with the light-fire meditation described above, the participants ingested a measured 5 mg dose via the snuffing method. After about twenty to thirty minutes, those who felt secure and wanted to go deeper could choose to take an additional dose of about 5–10 mg. The whole experience lasted about an hour and a half. Participants were encouraged to practice any one of the three serpentine meditations they had previously learned.

During the entire session recordings of meditative music with bells or gongs quietly played, as well as drawn-out chanting of the cosmic mantra *AUM*. Open-vowel toning and closed-mouth humming were practiced during the preparation phase and participants were encouraged to hum and tone quietly to themselves during the experience, harmonizing with the sounds of gongs and bells. I would add periodic reminders of centering and balancing awareness and the down-pouring light-fire meditation.

Ouroboros Experiences
Woman in her fifties, artist:

> When we practiced the ouroboros circulation of the light, there was a blending of ascending and descending energies, rising like a soft vapor, flowing downward like a fluid. It was an orgasmic sensation,

almost overwhelming. A feeling of a blending and merging of all the energies and currents of body, mind, and spirit. The movements of energy came in steps or waves, orgasmic waves, each wave like a volcanic explosion, dissolving finally into a oneness of matter and energy, the inner and the outer.

Man in his fifties, acupuncturist:

After listening to the guide's initial description and practicing the three different processes in the normal state of consciousness, I chose to work with the ouroboros serpent meditation with the entheogenic amplification. I visualized them as two connected serpent-like currents—one of them golden and the other one silvery—the mouth of one connected to the tail of the other. In my mind's eye they became two beautiful snakes with exquisite scales of multihued patterns of various golden and silvery shades. They moved and flowed slowly along the vertical axis of the body—called the "Conception Vessel" (yin) in the front and "Governor Vessel" (yang) along the back. Like two connected trains they flowed along these energetic pathways, recognized since the most ancient times.

As a healer trained in the ancient Chinese system of energy flows along meridian channels, this man first visualized the ouroboros serpent in front of him, and then, following the guidance and practice, experienced the two serpentine energy currents around the central axis inside his body. His attention focused and followed the flowing energy currents, and awareness of his physical body receded into background.

As the meditation and the medicine deepened, I lost awareness of my physical presence. I was completely transfixed by the ascending and descending serpentine currents. They became three-dimensional serpents, expanding to several times their original size. At first I was riding on the backs of the serpents, then I was gradually entering their bodies. My body image elongated as I merged with their forms. I became the serpents: my eyes were their eyes, my body their body. I was one continuous stream of energy, alternating between gold and silver over and over again. This current was flowing in a spherical motion within which was a vague awareness of my human body. The ouroboros circular flow of energy accelerated more and more until it was one continuous blur of light, circumnavigating my body. Suddenly, as if some kind of zipper was being pulled down, I was divided into two, each side falling down and away.

As the experience deepened, the human form was completely transcended, although he could still sense its presence in the background of awareness. He became a spherical energy form, which then split in half, revealing the archetypal androgynous twin soul within the human, with all the stories of his particular human life cycle seen in a flash as a whole. At the end he returned again to his familiar outer human form but with a deep and direct experience of his archetypal inner essence.

Two magnificent beings stood up as if emerging from inside a box that had been split in half. I knew immediately that these were my masculine and feminine selves, previously deeply hidden within me. I had the feeling they were twin souls, like two fetuses in one womb, living, growing, and maturing together through life. There was complete love and understanding for one another. I watched as they stood erect, stretching, looking around the room and then down toward me, as my physical body was lying on the ground. I recognized parts of myself in each. I saw the faces of my mother and sisters, my father and other males from his lineage. The faces were continuously morphing and changing. I saw myself as a boy, an adolescent, a young man, an older man. Emotionally, I felt waves of sadness, shame, pleasure, and pure joy. Sexual feelings, sensitivity and tenderness, courage and strength, washed through me, one after the other. I experienced time as standing still and moving at great speed, simultaneously. Eventually my male and female twins disappeared. I was whole again, complete, sitting in meditation, following the rhythm of my own breathing. I became aware of the music in the background, the sound of other people rustling around. Yet I felt permanently changed, healed in a fashion and in understanding of my human journey in a completely new way. The alchemical conception of the inner masculine and feminine in each of us became as real to me as night and day, as the sun and the moon.

Caduceus Experiences

In the following account, the experience started with powerful healing energy currents moving sinuously along the vertical axis of the body and then, with the mediation of her messenger bird ally, became a connection with a beloved, previously unknown, unborn human soul.

Woman in her fifties, health practitioner:

This was the night of the double helix. The first thing I noticed was a crow or raven sitting up high to my left at the very end of the room. The energy started pulsating and moving up my spine from the pelvis. As I was hearing the music coming from the speakers at both ends of the room, I noticed that the energy in my pelvis was also going back and forth across from each hip, in a bilateral pulsation. Then, as it moved up my spine I could feel the double helix around my spinal column, healing as it moved around and back and forth. I'm not sure for how long, but it went back and forth, around and down and up—healing everything in my body.

At some point I became aware of a small hawk above my head. It was the messenger and it allowed me to be with some souls in another realm. One was an unborn child, and I sensed we were communicating. I've never had contact with this soul before. I had tears and I felt we were deeply connected. I kept saying "I love you" over and over. It was a very profound experience, and I can still remember it very vividly, months afterwards.

In the following account, we can see how, even when the mind is preoccupied with doubts and feelings of inadequacy, once the deity spirit is accepted and received, a message of encouragement is conveyed along with a practice, tailored to the individual's level of perception and understanding.

Man in his thirties:

When we started the meditation with the Hermes staff, I was trying to bring the image of two serpents in my body, moving upward, while seeking contact with my Higher Self. I was full of stress and restlessness, thinking it was too hard for me. My mind was saying, "You can't do it." Suddenly I perceived the presence of Hermes, the deity. He took my hand and guided me. He showed me a bowl and silently encouraged me to put everything into it that was not important at this time. I noticed then that I was stuffed full of all kinds of information from news media, television, and the internet. I also noticed how many of my thoughts were concerned with worries, wishes, and problems that actually had nothing to do with the present and that were pulling me away from this moment. Hermes showed me or said that I could place all of these thought forms and images into the golden bowl. He said that if they were really important to me, I could take them out of the bowl and keep them for later. Thus he showed me and coached me on how to sort what was essential and what was just stuff.

In the following account we can see how the visualization of the caduceus progressed from perceiving the serpentine energy currents inside the body to perceiving one's self being inside the "staff"—which then became a vehicle for the practice of interdimensional travel.

Woman in her fifties:

As we started to work with the Hermes staff, I allowed myself to be "taken" by the medicine and visualized myself with the energy currents of the caduceus surrounding me. I was inside the staff itself, with the left and right wings beginning at my ears and extending downward behind my shoulders all the way to my lowest rib on each side. Mercurius or Hermes the deity then appeared at the foot of the mat where I was lying—a very tall, handsome, silvery, human-like figure, with wings on the sides of his head and his feet. He was gigantic. Then I began to sense the two uncoiled snakes, reminding me of images I'd seen of the DNA molecule, moving up and down the vertical axis of my body, creating a hollow cylindrical vehicle, which I knew was for space travel. Although my body was lying horizontally on the floor mat, not moving a muscle, I was inside the cylinder and felt myself begin to spin. Lifting off from the mat, I left this time-space dimension, traveling timelessly, feeling full, happy, peaceful, and very wise.

The following account makes clear how the experience triggered by the Hermetic practice and the entheogenic substance completely transcends the verbal. Although triggered by the prior verbal description and then the amplified practice, it became clear to this woman that during the experience itself, it was important to let go of any attempt at verbalization—that this would only block the experience. Afterward, the guiding intelligence of Hermes that she had connected with could help her verbalize an experience full of paradox and seemingly impossible opposites.

Woman in her fifties:

Practicing the Hermes caduceus process, with red-gold and silvery-white energy currents, I first perceived the tails of the two serpents in my sexual organs, with great heat spreading throughout the entire pelvic and abdominal cavity. It was explosion and implosion simultaneously, expanding and contracting with great power. It was an incredible feeling and sensation and as I tried to conceptualize it verbally the process stopped. Then an inner voice told me to stop trying to understand it mentally, just allow it to happen. The explosive sensation/feeling intensified to the point where I felt I couldn't take it anymore. There was a sensation of simultaneously dissolving and being drawn together. I recalled the alchemical motto the guide had mentioned: solve et coagula—*dissolve and coagulate. This was what I was experiencing. Then, as I focused awareness in the heart chakra space and the crossing of the solar and lunar energy currents here, I felt the energy streaming outward spherically. I was practicing letting the energy flow, rather than making it flow. It was a soft, expansive flowing simultaneously outward and inward. A sense of being inside all life and all life being inside me. Then again the dissolving and centering, explosion and implosion simultaneously, rhythmically alternating and flowing with my in-breath and out-breath.*

Asclepius Serpent Staff Experiences

In the following account, a physician connected with the archetypal divine physician came to accept, at a very deep level, the inevitable and paradoxical challenge of the healer—of working with people on the knife's edge of life and death. Asclepius taught him and showed him that these matters of life and death were not unique personal failings but inevitable aspects of the healer's pathway. In the second part of his journey he came into contact with three divine healer spirits, who helped him with some personal issues.

Man in his fifties, physician:

Over the years I've done a lot of inner work with grief and self-judgment related to people who have died while under my care. I've experienced deep healing as a result of this work, but still I carried the idea that being a good physician was one thing, and mistakes and bad outcomes were a departure from that—they were my personal failings. When I connected with the image and the energy of Asclepius, god of medicine, in my body, my first thought was that he could help me with the former so that there would be less of the latter—I still related to this as a polarity. As I felt the serpentine energy of Asclepius moving up my spine I suddenly had the realization, "Of course you've had these experiences with the pain of death, loss, mistakes, fear, tragic outcomes, the challenge of staying focused when the stakes are so high, not to be overwhelmed by the intensity of emotions just beneath the surface, what it means to step into the responsibility for helping people who are sick, injured or dying." Asclepius was essentially saying, "Do you think I don't know all of this? This is an inevitable part of being a physician, not some unique personal failing!" There was no hint of dismissing or minimizing the weight of these experiences, only deep acceptance and acknowledgment of what has been and what is—the reality, the beauty, the intensity, and the challenges of this archetype in my life. A weight was lifted from me. I felt tremendous gratitude for the support and acceptance of this wise and powerful ally.

Then three more physicians arrived beside me. Two of them appeared as shapes of energy, one to the right of my head and the other near my right hip. The third was in the shape of a bird-like figure that looked Mayan and was bending over my body on the right side of my torso. At first I felt some fear, heaviness, and emotional pain but also knew it was okay because this is what they were all working so intently to heal. As they worked I could feel the energy of Asclepius balancing my three brains—forebrain, limbic brain and reptilian brain. Polarities dissolved and I felt wholeness and the force of love.

In the following account, a woman psychotherapist, who had lifelong separation and boundary issues with her own mother, traced the mother-daughter difficulties back to the embryonic and fetal stages of her life, when her entire body was in toxic shock absorbed from her mother's body. She intuitively realized and practiced separating her sense of self from her mother's—not rejecting her mother but recognizing and affirming her own distinct identity as a breathing individual. A remembered connection with a totemic Bear spirit confirmed the beauty and integrity of both their souls.

Woman in her seventies, psychotherapist:

Before we began the process, as the guide was describing the three serpentine divinations, I was filled with pleasurable anticipation and curiosity. Then my feeling state changed abruptly into extreme death anxiety, as it often did when starting a healing divination, and I knew intuitively I would choose the Asclepius serpent staff to work with. I invited that serpent to come into my body and start its healing movement, which it did, gently and slowly. I "saw" at the cellular level that my embryonic body when in my mother's womb was completely permeated with terror. And I saw that my mother's cells were also all filled with this same fear. There was no boundary or difference between my mother's cells and mine. All the cells were filled with this fear of life. As we continued with the meditation I somehow knew that healing was taking place. I was taking hold of the residues of my mother's anxiety and moving them out of my body with each out-breath. The process was based on the power of intention, my willpower, the breath, and the light.

The process then continued and merged on all the different levels of my being—and finally dissolved into nothingness. This nothingness however was not nothing—it was a state of being, like a large heart field drawing everything toward itself and dissolution. A large brown bear appeared and was standing in front of me—Big Bear. Emerald green light poured from his paws and from his heart. I heard his voice: "Don't forget the old family traditions of healing." As I look back on this experience, I recognize it was an important

*piece of the whole process of dis-identifying with my mother. So that
I could see her for who she was as a person and also see the beauty of
the soul that she is. And therefore also connecting with my own soul.*

Not everyone who works with one of these healing deities or spirits, whether in human or serpentine form, necessarily visually perceives them. The woman in the following account, however, envisioned Asclepius as a wise old man, accompanied by his daughter Hygeia. The serpents from the old mythic temples of healing manifested as snakes, slithering all over her body but without eliciting any personal fear. She experienced the snakes as wise, intelligent beings, who responded to her requests for healing by moving physically through her body and triggering reintegration of painfully disconnected parts of her childhood.

Woman in her fifties:

As soon as I heard the name Asclepius, *I envisioned him with long
white curling hair and a robe of pale colors. His beautiful daughter
Hygeia sat beside him, and she began to lull me into sleep. Slowly,
snakes began to emerge from everywhere and surrounded me,
slithering all over me. I noticed that there was a "I'm supposed to
feel afraid" thought in my mind—but actually there was no fear.
I knew from somewhere deep inside that I just needed to keep
surrendering so that I could be healed. I asked for healing in my
right thigh, which had been cramping and bothering me for quite a
while. I saw and felt a knotted cord of energy from my thigh all the
way up into my left adrenal and kidney area. As it started to untwist
I began to see how my sexual energy had been shut down and shut
off. I was led to a powerful memory from the preadolescent time of*

my life. The twisted coils were the ambivalence I felt about staying with the innocence and protection offered by my grandmother and my fear of being with the raw masculine energy of my father. I let myself relax and sink into the deep healing peace of the Asclepius serpentine energy.

The man in the following account is a physician who had previously had some experience with 5-meo-DMT, inhaled through a vaporizer, as an amplifier of meditative or therapeutic insight. He thought it was interesting but had limited applicability because of the short time duration of ten to fifteen minutes. He said that he did not receive any significant insights from that experience. In the following experience, after preparatory meditations with the serpentine imagery of Hermes and Asclepius, he insufflated 5 mg, and twenty minutes later an additional 8 mg. A very powerful connection with Asclepius ensued in which he not only experienced the serpentine healing currents within himself but also was shown a further extension of the healing practice with the use of a staff.

Man in his fifties, psychiatrist:

Several minutes after insufflation I began to experience a very mild vibratory sensation. I felt calm, free of anxiety, and at no point encountered any dissociative phenomena. Although lying on my back with eyes closed, I was fully present in the room, alert, oriented, and able to briefly converse and describe some of my experience as it was occurring. While I normally do not consider myself to be particularly skilled at sustained guided imagery exercises, on this particular occasion I was able to establish a strong and persistent focus on the visualizations throughout the course of the experience.

Initially I tried to perceive the caduceus of Hermes but was not able to envision the two entwined snakes. I then shifted my focus to the vision of a single snake wrapping itself around a staff, an image I was effectively able to sustain for the duration of the experience.

My initial experience with the visualization was of the snake ascending the staff, which then transformed to the snake ascending my central core. The snake would turn into energy circuits, rising, undulating, and alternating at times between silver and gold conduits of energy, emanating an ethereal light. I was fully relaxed, engaged, and able to release into the experience.

A very clear and unexpected vision began to manifest of an elderly man wearing flowing white robes, with a long white beard and long white hair cascading down his back. He appeared strong, with a regal bearing, standing erect and with an intense focus looking straight ahead. With his right hand, he held a vertical staff around which a serpent was wrapping itself in an ascending manner, with its tail at the bottom and head at the top of the staff. As this vision unfolded, I realized I was having a vision of Asclepius, the Greek god of healing. He then began to turn the staff from a straight upright position to a horizontal 90 degrees, directing healing energy through the staff toward my chronic orthopedic injuries and then to a recent surgical site. He would systematically move the serpent-entwined staff over my body, particularly toward points of somatic vulnerability, catalyzing waves of subtle healing energy.

With Asclepius on my right side, a new vision began to emerge on my left side of my father, who had been a great physician in his day. In the vision, my father looked as he did in his prime, in his thirties and forties, with a quiet power and steady gaze and not as the ravaged appearance manifested at the end of his life. I suddenly realized that my father had himself been a student of Asclepius, and that I and my younger brother, who is also a physician, were students of our father, and that we were all also students of Asclepius.

The experience was one of personal healing, as well as an initiation into the art of healing, instilling in me the archaic knowledge necessary to facilitate healing in patients and others with whom I interact. Throughout this experience, which lasted approximately three quarters of an hour, I remained entirely conscious, lucid, and feeling in control. Afterwards I felt calm and grounded, with a sense of being blessed with a profound connection to a lineage of which I had not previously been fully cognizant. All in all, it was a remarkable healing experience as well as an initiation into the most ancient healing arts.

◆ ◆ ◆

The most significant conclusion one can draw from the methods and experiences recounted in this chapter is that certain key serpent *symbols* can also be seen as coded instructions for healing and meditative practices. The particular configuration of staff and serpent images, when superimposed on an image of the human body, reveals an emblem of instructions for subtle energy practices—a kind of summary manual of alchemical yogic practices of healing and visioning. The key to the yogic healing use of the serpent imagery is to place the symbolic form inside one's own subjective three-dimensional body image. If you just look at the two-dimensional picture outside of yourself, even with Jungian "active imagination," the serpent image will remain just that—an image in the mind.

In the entheogenic sessions in which the serpentine visions occurred, I did not guide the visualizations. I described the alchemical yogic practice associated with each of the serpentine images and guided a practice session of using the chosen symbolic image as an energy process in one's own body. After ingesting the amplifying substance, the individuals themselves chose whichever of the three serpentine imagery processes they resonated with the most, and practiced it silently while concentrating on their experience. I was myself astonished by the depth and diversity of the experiences that occurred.

I hope I have made it clear that there is nothing definitive that connects visions of serpents with any particular psychoactive medicine—they can occur with any medicine or no medicine at all, for example with shamanic drumming journeys. The medicine, with the preparation, acts only as an amplifier of perception and awareness. The key is always the intention fortified with preparation and practice. But even with preparatory meditations on serpent imagery there is no guarantee that such visions will occur. From my collection of accounts, I have of course always selected the most impressive examples.

The experiences related here show that there is a special power and efficacy to working with the classic symbolic serpentine processes. I believe that this efficacy stems from their extensive history of use. Many thousands, perhaps millions, in the ancient world practiced and experienced the healing methods encoded in these serpentine metaphors. To use Rupert Sheldrake's concepts, one could say there are powerful *morphogenetic* fields associated with these figures and symbols that have been built up over time as a function of repetition and practice. In this way, we can honor the living deity spirits that support the healing arts—the kundalini and ouroboros serpents, Hermes/Mercurius and his twin serpent staff, Asclepius and his divine daughter Hygeia.

Conclusions

In the introduction I pointed out how patterns of karma from present or previous lifetimes can affect our consciousness and our sense of self like hidden undercurrents as we swim in the multiple streams of our lives. Such turbulent undercurrents of psychic energy may have originated in the prenatal or even preconception period, as exemplified in chapters 3 and 4 on the unexpected consequences of abortion.

Karmic undercurrents, recognized or not, may persist across generations of familial ancestry. The stories in chapters 6, 7, and 8 exemplify how traumatic patterns in the family matrix, passed on unconsciously, can be healed when both the strengths and the weaknesses of the ancestral lineages are recognized and assimilated.

The expanded worldview that I have come to develop on the basis of my own observations, consistent with the worldview of Eastern and indigenous cultures, recognizes that karmic patterns may extend not just through ancestral lineages but also across different incarnations in different times and places. Like other psychotherapists who work with past-life therapy, I tend to look for reincarnational patterns when biographical, prenatal, or ancestral causality seems insufficient. In chapters 9 through 12, I related healings and resolutions that occurred when painful residues from a past life could be acknowledged and processed.

The principle of karma implies that not only the difficulties but also the strengths and talents of our present life may be causally connected with previous lifetimes. Positive patterns carried over from other lives may not necessarily be recognized as such, but instead may resonate like subtle overtone harmonics from the archetypal dimensions, adding depth and spiritual meaning to our experience. In chapter 2 I relate how the spiritual dimensions of a relationship quandary could be recognized and resolved through the use of a fourfold mandala or medicine wheel. In chapter 5, contact with an unexpected shamanic ally led to a profound healing of ancient wounds. Chapter 6 relates the story of how remembering a previously discounted ancestor connection led to a deepened spirituality.

As related in chapters 13 and 14, even situations of malignant intrusions from disembodied entities can be dealt with and healed if we invoke the assistance of our shamanic spirit allies and practice standing steady in the lighted center of our beingness. Those stories as well as the serpentine healing visions related in chapter 15 and the healing stories throughout the book show how the integration of alchemical, shamanic, and yogic practices along with the selective use of entheogenic and empathogenic substances can open up new possibilities of growth and healing.

If we can expand our worldview to both recognize and evoke the subtle spiritual dimensions of our experience, analogous to the ethereal overtones of a piece of music, we may also come to a deeper understanding of the hidden karmic undercurrents that can divert us from our life purpose and disrupt harmonious familial relations.

Bibliography

Breggin, Peter. *Toxic Psychiatry*. New York: St. Martin's Press, 1991.

Crabtree, Adam. *Multiple Man: Explorations in Possession and Multiple Personality*. New York: Praeger, 1985.

Dass, Ram, and Ralph Metzner, with Gary Bravo. *Birth of a Psychedelic Culture: Conversations about Leary, the Harvard Experiments, Millbrook, and the Sixties*. Santa Fe, N.Mex.: Synergetic Press, 2010.

Foster, Steven, with Meredith Little. *The Four Shields: The Initiatory Seasons of Human Nature*. Big Pine, Calif.: Lost Borders Press, 1999.

Hellinger, Bert. *On Life & Other Paradoxes: Aphorisms and Little Stories from Bert Hellinger*. Translated by Ralph Metzner. Phoenix, Ariz.: Zeig, Tucker & Theissen, 2002.

Laing, R. D. *The Politics of Experience*. New York: Pantheon, 1967.

Leary, Timothy, Ralph Metzner, and Richard Alpert. *The Psychedelic Experience: A Manual Based on the Tibetan Book of the Dead*. New Hyde Park, N.Y.: University Books, 1964.

Metzner, Ralph. *Allies for Awakening: Guidelines for Productive and Safe Experiences with Entheogens*. Berkeley, Calif.: Green Earth Foundation and Regent Press, 2015.

———. "A Note on the Treatment of LSD Psychosis: A Case Report," *Psychotherapy: Theory, Research and Therapy*, 6, no. 3 (1969): 201–5.

———. *The Ayahuasca Experience: A Sourcebook on the Sacred Vine of Spirits.* Rochester, Vt.: Park Street Press, 2014.

———. *Ecology of Consciousness: The Alchemy of Personal, Collective, and Planetary Transformation.* Oakland, Calif.: Reveal Press—New Harbinger Publications, 2017.

———. *The Ecstatic Adventure.* New York: Macmillan, 1968.

———. *Eye of the Seeress—Voice of the Poet: Visions—Poems—Prayers.* Berkeley, Calif.: Green Earth Foundation and Regent Press, 2011.

———. *Sacred Mushroom of Visions—Teonanácatl: A Sourcebook on the Psilocybin Mushroom.* Rochester, Vt.: Park Street Press, 2005.

———. *The Toad and the Jaguar.* Berkeley, Calif.: Green Earth Foundation and Regent Press, 2013.

———. *The Well of Remembrance: Rediscovering the Earth Wisdom Myths of Northern Europe.* Boston: Shambhala Publications, 1994.

Narby, Jeremy. *The Cosmic Serpent: DNA and the Origins of Knowledge.* New York: Jeremy P. Tarcher, 1998.

Sheldrake, Rupert. *The Presence of the Past: Morphic Resonance and the Habits of Nature.* London: Icon Books, 2011.

Stevenson, Ian. *Cases of the Reincarnation Type.* 2 vols. Charlottesville: University of Virginia Press, 1975–78.

Index

Other Books by Ralph Metzner

Ecology of Consciousness

Allies for Awakening

The Toad and the Jaguar

Birth of a Psychedelic Culture
(with Ram Dass & Gary Bravo)

The Roots of War and Domination

The Six Pathways of Destiny

Sacred Vine of Spirits: Ayahuasca

Sacred Mushroom of Visions: Teonanácatl

Green Psychology

The Unfolding Self

The Well of Remembrance

Through the Gateway of the Heart
(with Sophia Adamson and Padma Catell)

Know Your Type

Maps of Consciousness

The Ecstatic Adventure

The Psychedelic Experience
(with Timothy Leary & Richard Alpert)

Books of Related Interest

The Ayahuasca Experience
A Sourcebook on the Sacred Vine of Spirits
Edited by Ralph Metzner, Ph.D.

Sacred Mushroom of Visions: Teonanácatl
A Sourcebook on the Psilocybin Mushroom
Edited by Ralph Metzner, Ph.D.

DMT: The Spirit Molecule
A Doctor's Revolutionary Research into the Biology
of Near-Death and Mystical Experiences
by Rick Strassman, M.D.

Psychedelic Marine
A Transformational Journey from Afghanistan to the Amazon
by Alex Seymour

The Psychedelic Explorer's Guide
Safe, Therapeutic, and Sacred Journeys
by James Fadiman, Ph.D.

Cannabis and Spirituality
An Explorer's Guide to an Ancient Plant Spirit Ally
Edited by Stephen Gray
Foreword by Julie Holland, M.D.

Dreaming Wide Awake
Lucid Dreaming, Shamanic Healing, and Psychedelics
by David Jay Brown

Psychedelic Healing
The Promise of Entheogens for Psychotherapy and Spiritual
Development
by Neal M. Goldsmith, Ph.D.

INNER TRADITIONS • BEAR & COMPANY
P.O. Box 388
Rochester, VT 05767
1-800-246-8648
www.InnerTraditions.com

Or contact your local bookseller